Masters Running Guide

**Beyond Fitness:
How to get in shape
to perform, for the best
years of your life.**

by Hal Higdon

Author: Fitness After Forty

The
Masters
Running
Guide

Beyond Fitness:
How to get in shape
to perform, for the best
years of your life.

by Hal Higdon
Author: Fitness After Forty

Portions of this book appeared previously in *Runner's World*.

ISGN: 0-910725-05-5

Library of Congress Catalog Card Number 90-60785
Printed in the U.S.A.
First Printing: May, 1990

Dedicated to David H. R. Pain, founder for us all. If David
hadn't decided at age 44 to switch sports from handball to
jogging, there might not be any masters runners to guide.

OTHER BOOKS BY HAL HIGDON

The Union vs. Dr. Mudd
Heroes of the Olympics
Pro Football, USA
The Horse that Played Center Field
The Business Healers
On the Run from Dogs and People
Thirty Days in May
Champions of the Tennis Courts
The Electronic Olympics
Finding the Groove
Find the Key Man
The Last Series
The Crime of the Century
Six Seconds to Glory
Showdown at Daytona
Summer of Triumph
Fitness After Forty
Beginner's Running Guide
Hitting, Pitching, and Fielding
Runner's Cookbook
Johnny Rutherford
The Marathoners
The Team that Played in the Space Bowl

CONTENTS

Introduction: WE DO THINGS DIFFERENTLY

Early spring. Nineteen eighty-nine. Hal Higdon was on the phone. We talked about the upcoming World Veterans' Championships in Eugene, Oregon, then drifted into the usual runner's banter:

"Who's running well in your area?"

"How's your training coming?"

"Doing any racing?"

Alas, assorted ailments had sidelined me again. I commented to Hal that I wish I was smart enough to avoid injuries. I read everything I can about training, but with the exception of *National Masters News*, most fitness articles and books concentrate on younger runners–or at least fail to provide specific advice for the growing numbers of masters athletes.

Anyone over age 40 who has tried walking, jogging, running or various other fitness activities knows that what worked in our youths doesn't work for us now. Our bodies respond differently. We're less flexible. We can't recover from intense workouts as rapidly as before. Injuries heal more slowly. Despite our best efforts, performances inevitably decline. "What we need," I mused, "is a running and fitness book written exclusively for people over age 40. A book that would offer help and advice to *masters* participants, based on the fact that we do things differently than when we were younger."

Higdon said that he had been thinking the same.

"So why don't you write such a book?" I asked.

I consider Hal Higdon one of the world's most knowledgeable masters writers. He's a full-time freelance writer. He's also a three-time World Vets champion. I told Hal: "Who's better qualified to write a book on masters running? You write it. *National Masters News* will publish it."

Higdon eventually agreed to do: "Masters Running Guide."

In it, Hal has combined his experiences as an open and masters runner with the latest sportsmedicine research on athletes over age 40.

He describes masters sports and discusses the safety of intensive competition for older athletes, particularly after the death of Jim Fixx. He talks about basic fitness, getting in shape, and what interests most masters athletes: *How to perform*!

He offers insights into training and how to avoid injuries. He provides what I consider one of the most fascinating chapters, that on maintaining mobility through flexibility drills and massage. He talks about diet and good health habits. He closes the book with a chapter on the 1989 World Veterans' Games in Eugene, Oregon, an expanded version of an article that appeared originally in the December 1989 issue of *Runner's World*, a magazine he serves as Senior Writer. "It's not going to help anybody run faster," concedes Higdon, "but it's one of my favorite pieces of writing."

I agree. There's also a useful appendix that describes the nuts and bolts of the sport: publications, camps, equipment, and more. If you're new to masters running, it will ease your entry into the sport.

This is the first book written exclusively for the masters performer since Higdon's best-selling "Fitness After Forty" was published in 1977. It's a compact, state-of-the-art, how-to-do-it guide for anyone over age 40.

The National Masters News is proud to publish Hal Higdon's "Masters Running Guide." I hope you enjoy it and hope also that it helps to improve your health, your fitness, your performances and your good mood.

Happy reading.

Al Sheahen, Publisher/Editor
National Masters News

1. MASTERS OF THEIR FATES

The air was electric with energy inside French Field House on the campus of Ohio State University. French Field House is a massive, shed-like building, from whose tall ceiling hang flags for each of the Big Ten schools. On this April weekend, hundreds of colorfully garbed athletes filled the indoor arena, sprinting swiftly around its rubberized, 200 meter track, hurling heavy shots, leaping lightly over bars and into pits.

These were not collegians. The grey hair of the athletes betrayed their years. Many had weathered faces though few showed the bulging paunch or bent shoulders ordinarily associated with aging. Indeed, viewed in action, this group of aged competitors displayed youthful vitality, literally *glowed* with it. They had come to Columbus, Ohio to compete in the U.S.National Masters Indoor Track and Field Championships of The Athletic Congress (T.A.C.). For many, it was the climax of the indoor season; for others, a prelude to the World Veterans' Championships later during the summer of 1989.

As the gun sounded, activating a bevy of over-40 sprinters, I overheard a reporter ask San Diego attorney David Pain, 67, whether those competing hoped to improve their longevity by doing so.

Pain, founder of the masters movement and competitor that day (unplaced) at 1500 meters, smiled tolerantly at a question he had heard asked frequently. "Longevity?" he replied. "Most of these runners are too busy having fun to worry about longevity."

The percentage of older people is steadily increasing. Nearly 12 per cent of the United States population is over

65. By the year 2050, nearly 22 percent–67.1 million people–will be in that category. At the Eighth World Veterans' Championships in Eugene, Oregon in 1989, 4951 older athletes from 58 nations participated. The number of athletes was more than compete in the track events at the Olympics.

Masters competition is on the rise for a simple reason: we're all getting older. The number of years we live has increased steadily, from an average lifespan of 26 years in the Stone Age, to 36 in the Middle Ages, to 47 at the beginning of this century. Today, the average American man lives 70.3 years; the average woman, 78. Americans might logically use the old gag line: "If I knew I was going to live this long, I'd have taken better care of myself."

The aging process remains a mystery. We can describe the "normal" changes attributed to aging–wrinkled skin, gray hair, stiffer joints, and so forth–but those changes do not affect everyone at the same rate. Scientists lately have begun to research how much of so-called aging is the inevitable consequence of the passage of years and how much can be altered by factors such as diet and exercise.

Inevitably, researchers point to "exercise habits" as a major factor affecting how we survive into old age. Indeed, many of the problems of aging are not caused by disease, but by *disuse*! Or to use another term popular with scientists: de-training. We allow ourselves to get out of shape, to rust, to grow older than our chronological years. By running, by swimming, by cycling, by skiing, by walking, by lifting weights, by stretching, by staying in shape, we extend the years of our youth.

Exercise scientists have begun to research the apparent hardiness of older people who exercise. One such study at the Stanford University School of Medicine identified runners over 50 as having, "less musculoskeletal disability and better cardiovascular fitness than non-runners the same age." In addition, runners weighed less, took fewer medications, lost fewer work days, perceived their health as better and saw physicians less frequently.

A good example is Paul Spangler, M.D., a retired surgeon from San Luis Obispo, California. Dr. Spangler, 91, holds most of the world records from 400 meters through the marathon for athletes over 80. He holds more world and American records than any other athlete. He was the oldest finisher in the Bay to Breakers race in San Francisco for ten consecutive years. He won six gold medals and one silver, while setting four world age-90-and-over records, at the "World Vets" meet in Eugene. Dr. Spangler also wins swimming races and makes no secret of his success: "You simply live longer than your competition."

Although Dr. Spangler, once a Navy captain, is a veteran of three wars, the World Veterans' Championships is not for former servicemen. "Veterans" is the international identification for athletes over age 40. Within the United States, the term most often used is "masters," with "senior" a variation for those past 55. Women have been allowed to compete as masters at 35, and age-group competition in some sports (notably swimming) starts as early as 19 (25 internationally). Regardless of where you draw the line, competition exclusively for older athletes is on the rise.

Dr. Spangler began running after he retired at age 67, "to improve my health." Burwell Jones, M.D., on the other hand, set a world record and competed in the 1952 Olympics as a teenager. A dermatologist from Sarasota, Florida, Dr. Jones, 56, continues to compete in the pool and also on the golf course. In addition to dominating his age class in swim competition, he is two-time champion of the American Medical Golf Association tournament (also known as the Desert Medical Classic), held on the Bob Hope course in Palm Springs, California. "I usually alternate years between golf and swimming," says Dr. Jones.

Masters sports is merely one facet of the fitness boom. Barbara L. Drinkwater, Ph.D., past president of the American College of Sports Medicine, offers that organization's endorsement of regular exercise: "No matter what your age, no matter how long you've been sedentary, if you become active, you can improve your physiological function and delay–if not prevent–many problems of aging."

Drinkwater, a member of the Department of Medicine at Pacific Medical Center, stays in shape by hiking and gardening near her home outside Seattle, Washington. Non-competitive, she considers those activities perfectly adequate for fitness. To stay healthy, you don't necessarily need to throw javelins or ski slalom gates. Kenneth H. Cooper, M.D., whose best-seller "Aerobics" helped launch the fitness boom, agrees. He considers 10-15 miles a week of walking or jogging sufficient. "Any more than that and you're exercising for reasons other than fitness," suggests Dr. Cooper.

But neither Drinkwater nor Dr. Cooper would discourage Drs. Spangler or Jones from their competitive efforts as masters. Indeed, some research indicates that competition that involves aggressive training provides a *higher* degree of fitness than Cooper's guideline or the 15-60 minutes of exercise 3-5 days a week suggested by the American College of Sports Medicine as good for our health.

Michael L. Pollock, Ph.D., director of the Center for Exercise Science at the University of Florida, helped design the A.C.S.M. guidelines above. Pollock has been studying a group of two dozen masters track athletes, including myself, since 1971. Periodically, Pollock brings our hearty group of oldsters back to his laboratory for retesting. All of us have continued to exercise. As a group, we exhibit lower body fat and a higher fitness level (as measured by treadmill tests) than the general population.

But in a recent retesting, a schism developed within our group. Eleven among the 24 demonstrated a higher level of fitness and less body fat. What was the difference? Those 11 had continued to *compete!* Pollock reported: "The group that continued to train at the same level generally maintained their cardiorespiratory fitness, while the other group did not. Even though the noncompetitive group decreased significantly, they are still at a very high level of aerobic capacity."

Studies at the University of Illinois at Chicago confirms Pollock's point. Robert C. Hickson, Ph.D. identifies intensity as playing an important role in maintaining fitness. Yet not everybody is equipped either physically or psychologically to train at high intensity. Obvious dangers exist. Hickson admits that his subjects were highly motivated volunteers, carefully screened to avoid risks of heart attack. Pollock notes that intensity frightens many beginners. He cautions against the injuries that too-intense programs can produce. "When you exercise more than 4-5 days a week, injuries increase exponentially," warns Pollock.

Is that true? Masters athletes seemingly should be more prone to injury than their younger peers. Muscle tears presumably should occur more easily and heal more slowly once you pass middle age. There is also the specter of sudden death lurking over the age-group playing fields.

Surprisingly, heart attacks in masters competition rarely occur, and you would be as likely to see an athlete stopped by a pulled hamstring in a high school track meet than at the World Vets meet. Masters athletes seem more capable of knowing the limitations of their bodies. Experience teaches us how to train more intelligently and avoid the mistakes of youth. Another interpretation, however, may be that those most liable to suffer injuries get eliminated at lower levels. And those at *highest* risk never start to exercise, much less compete.

Yet some athletes never seem to slow down. Bill Shoemaker, was 54 in 1986 when he won his fourth Kentucky Derby victory, his 8537th career win. Asked by reporters whether it was not unusual for a man his age to win the Derby, the Shoe smiled as he replied: "I'm like good, old Kentucky bourbon. I improve with age."

Dick Simon, 55, from Capistrano Beach, California defied common knowledge that auto racing is a high-risk sport by continuing to compete in the Indianapolis 500. Simon first drove the Indianapolis 500 in 1970 as a 36-year-old "rookie." Underfinanced, often forced to use inferior equipment, Simon nevertheless made the starting field of this prestigious race every year but two from 1970 through 1988.

Ironically, he achieved his greatest success after turning 50. In a sport where mechanical, rather than physical, breakdown is the most common cause of defeat, finishing is often the greatest accomplishment. Between 1986 and 1988 at Indy, Simon finished each year, even while giving much of his attention to the cars of younger drivers on the Dick Simon Racing Team. In 1987 at age 53, and again in 1988 at age 54, Simon became the oldest driver ever to run at Indy. In 1987, he ran 213.7 m.p.h. at Michigan International, the fastest lap ever run at that race track. "I would love to win Indy," he says. "I've come close several times, but 'close' doesn't go into the record books."

Shoemaker and Simon are anomalies: athletes who compete on equal terms with those younger. Most masters athletes find it easier to compete against others their same age. The Professional Golf Association Senior Tour provides a showcase for golfers over 50, including Chi Chi Rodriguez of Naples, Florida. Though top-ranked as a pro when younger, Rodriguez never earned as much money as he did in 1986, his first year as a senior: he won three tournaments and $400,000. In 1987, Rodriguez shot 12 consecutive rounds under 70, winning a record four straight titles on the Senior Tour. "I've found the Fountain of Youth," said Rodriguez.

But most masters athletes are unknown athletes competing in sports where they win medals instead of money. Father of the masters movement is David H. R. Pain, a San Diego attorney and handball player, who began jogging in 1966 at age 44 because it was troublesome locating partners of equal ability. He enjoyed his new sport, but missed the competitive aspects of his old sport, which included masters competition in ten-year age brackets. Talking a track promoter into adding a "masters mile" for runners over 40, Pain soon found himself organizing a national masters track and field meet and leading a group overseas in 1972 for age-group competitions in Great Britain, Germany and Scandinavia. Three years later, in 1975, the World Veterans' Championships was founded in Toronto, Canada. The 1989 event in Eugene was the eighth biennial world meet. It included all track and field events contested in the Olympic Games plus a few more. Masters permitted women in long distance events well before the International Olympic Committee did.

Athletes in other sports saw the success of the track masters and began to found, and expand, their own sporting events at national and world levels. Masters competition in swimming began in 1971; in cross country skiing, 1982. Bicyclists have had age-group races at their national championships since 1972.

The secret of senior sports is allowing athletes to compete in age groups against peers. Masters competition began with ten-year age groups, but five-year splits soon became the norm, recognizing the fact that even the fittest 49-year-old has difficulty competing equally with a youngster just turned 40. Unlike the general population, masters athletes rejoice at getting older—crossing a decade—because it opens up new vistas of competition.

With masters competition in all sports growing, organizers have found it necessary to sub-divide further to keep numbers at a manageable level. In 1987, the U.S. National Senior Olympics offered competition open only to those over 55. Remarkably, 2800 athletes appeared in St. Louis on the same grounds at Washington University used for the 1904 Olympic Games to participate in ten different sports. Track and field was most popular with 900 competitors, but also on the schedule were archery and golf.

Senior Olympic competitors had qualified at regional events held earlier in the year. Arizona had 196 entrants. The state of New Mexico supported its qualifiers with a grant of $25,000. At the opening ceremonies, they appeared nattily attired in red suits with gold trim. "The Parade of States demonstrated that there was a lot of state pride," commented U.S.N.S.O. president Ken Marshall, overjoyed at the success of this first national multi-sport championship event for athletes over 55. (The second such event was held again in St. Louis during June, 1989 with 3396 competitors; the third is scheduled for Syracuse, New York in 1991.)

During the beginnings of the masters movements, competitors in the oldest age groups were rare. It was not unusual for medals for those in their 70s and 80s to go unclaimed. Some competitors would walk (or jog) away from track meets with as many as a dozen gold medals, earned by merely entering events in which there were no other competitors. Women masters–discriminated against as athletes when young–were scarce.

But as the masters movement has matured, more and more athletes have begun to move into the older brackets. And more women have appeared. Encouragingly, the Senior Olympics attracted the largest numbers in the 60-64 age group. In 1987 and 1989, women comprised 38 and 37 per cent of competitors respectively. Here is the breakdown of participants by age and sex in 1989:

Age group	Male	Female	Combined
55-59	383	210	593
60-64	542	355	897
65-69	502	305	807
70-74	357	207	564
75-79	212	126	338
80-84	98	64	162
Totals	2126	1270	3396
	63%	37%	

In swimming at the 1987 meet, the 50 meter free style attracted 53 female entrants at age 65-69. In track, multiple heats were necessary to choose finalists in most sprint events. Swimming, bowling, horseshoes and table tennis were the three sports most popular with women.

The oldest competitor in 1987 was Robert Drewery, 93, of Cincinnati, Ohio, who only began running five years earlier. Drewery participated in the 100 and 400 meter dashes, but, alas, failed to win a medal since he was forced to compete against youngsters in the 80-plus division. (In contrast, the World Vets meet includes five-year brackets all the way through 95-99, and probably will add 100-plus as soon as the first centenarian appears.)

Growth in the masters movement has been hit and miss. A previous "Senior Olympics" in Southern California that included athletes as young as 25 proved successful through the 1970s, but eventually disappeared. A National Sports Festival for over-40 athletes in Philadelphia in 1982 was discontinued after its insurance company sponsor withdrew support. Organizers of a so-called "World Masters Games" for over-30 athletes in Toronto in 1985 clashed with international sanctioning bodies and fled after reportedly incurring a cash deficit of several million dollars. Similar problems plagued a 1989 sequel in Denmark.

Still, the Olympic Games were not an instant hit either. When Baron Pierre de Coubertin revived them in Athens, Greece in 1896, the American team consisted mostly of a few Eastern college athletes wealthy enough to pay their way. The 1904 Olympics in St. Louis attracted mainly American competitors. Only in ensuing decades did the Olympic Games grow in status and prestige, and only in 1984 in Los Angeles did Peter Ueberroth figure out how to run them at a profit. Cities in a half dozen countries are bidding for the privilege to host the Olympics in 1996, the 100th anniversary year.

Nobody yet has discovered how to make a profit from masters sports. Other than friends and relatives, few spectators appear to watch masters competition–and many competitors prefer it that way. The media gives masters sports only passing attention; when reporters appear, they most often seek human interest angles rather than reporting the competition straight. Reporters more familiar with football and basketball statistics have a difficult time evaluating times by sprinters one to two generations older, and two to three seconds slower, than Carl Lewis.

Often it is the oldest competitors who draw the most attention. At early world championships, Duncan MacLean, a Scot and one-time understudy to the famed singer Sir Harry Lauder, attracted attention by running the 100 meter dash while in his 90s. A vigorous man, he was the only competitor that age and had to run against two youngsters in their 80s at the first World Vets in 1975. He lost– but we all won.

At the 1987 World Vets in Melbourne, Australia, three competitors appeared for the 90-94 100 meter dash and one for 95-99. In that ultimate category, Prithvi Azad Singh of India ran 100 meters in 39 seconds for his gold medal. I was both competing in the meet and covering it for *Runner's World*. After Singh's race, I drifted over to the circle of reporters surrounding him on the track.

Through an interpreter, Singh described himself as a follower of Mahatma Gandhi. He had spent time in prisons in both India and the Soviet Union because of his revolutionary activities. "I once ran to stay out of jail," Singh explained. "Now I run for fitness."

Fitness! That's the catch-phrase. Usually, it's adequate for satisfying the curiosity of reporters facing deadlines. Supposedly it's why we run and jump and throw. But in all honesty--as masters pioneer David Pain well understood--older athletes compete for reasons that go well beyond fitness.

2. HOW SAFE ARE SENIOR SPORTS?

It was late on a Friday, July 20, 1984. Checking into a motel in northern Vermont, the traveler unpacked quickly and changed into shorts and running shoes. Fatigued after a long drive from Cape Cod, he planned to relax with a run before dinner. He set off down the road, happy in an activity he did daily.

Soon after, a passing motorcyclist noticed someone lying beside the road. It was the traveler. He wasn't moving. State police arrived quickly, but he was dead of a heart attack at age 52.

I learned of the traveler's death the following afternoon.Walking near my home, I barely noticed an approaching jogger. "Did you hear about Jim Fixx?" the jogger said in passing. "He died of a heart attack."

As a fellow runner I was surprised. James F. Fixx was the man who seemed to have invented running, a sport that was going to lengthen all our lives. "The Complete Book of Running," which Jim wrote in 1977, sold more than one million copies and launched not merely the running boom, but the fitness boom in many sports. Not merely runners, but also cyclists, swimmers, skiers, and other recreational athletes owe their active lifestyles to the positive climate created by Fixx's successful book.

I remembered Jim Fixx as an energetic and friendly man. At age 35 in 1967, Jim weighed 220 pounds and smoked two packs of cigarettes a day. He started running partly to prevent the heart attack that had killed his father at a young age. Soon Jim was slim and trim, the picture of good health. Now he was dead, participating in the very activity supposed to protect him.

Ironically, Fixx joked about the dangers of his sport. In a follow-up book "Jackpot," he offered an anecdote about a man who told a friend about this great book. The man couldn't recall the title, but everybody died at the end. "Oh," said the friend. "It must have been 'The Complete Book of Running.'"

How safe is masters sport? Vigorous activities such as running, swimming, cycling and skiing might be okay for highly conditioned, competitive athletes striving for Olympic glory, but what about the rest of us? Should we begin (or continue) competing past 40? Perhaps we should reduce our commitment to sport. Maybe it would be wise at least to avoid the most stressful endurance activities, such as marathons and triathlons. The thought of people in their 50s and 60s pole vaulting or putting the shot makes many insurance adjusters nervous. Running the 3000 meter steeplechase makes *me* nervous, despite two World Vets titles in that event. Masters steeplechasers are required to leap the same height barriers used in the Olympics. At the 1989 World Vets, I balked at the second barrier and walked off the track, having failed to complete one lap. The risk of injury seemed too high for one more medal hung around my neck.

Running lost some of its fad appeal after Fixx's death in 1984. That incident created a backlash, causing people to pause and consider whether running was an appropriate fitness activity. Jane Brody, health columnist for the New York *Times*, says she no longer advises running for older people. Others warn that running may damage the knees, feet, arches, hips, back, and eventually cause arthritis.

In "The Exercise Myth," Henry Solomon, M.D., a New York cardiologist, claimed that, based on the number of Americans jogging or exercising, as many as 40,000 men and 50,000 women a year may trigger heart attacks by running, or engaging in other fitness activities. Dr. Solomon would identify Jim Fixx's death as not an anomaly, but rather an anticipated occurrence.

Common sense tells us that fitness devotees are not dropping dead in anywhere near those epidemic numbers, otherwise cries would rise to have fitness banned—or at least have warnings printed on sports shoe boxes. Dr. Cooper says that if exercise were as dangerous as Dr. Solomon claimed, "I would have written 'The Exercise Myth' myself." Actually, deaths from heart attacks have declined 30 per cent during the period since 1968 when running went from a cult sport to one of mass appeal. Members of Dr. Cooper's Aerobics Center in Dallas have clocked seven million miles since 1971. "Over five thousand runners have participated in running those miles," says Dr. Cooper, "and there were only two nonfatal heart attacks and one fatality during that time."

Similarly, Stephen Van Camp, M.D., medical director at San Diego State, surveyed 167 cardiac rehabilitation programs involving 51,000 patients who exercised 2,350,000 hours. He identified only four fatalities, one every 800,000 patient hours. David Siscovick, M.D. of the department of medicine at the University of North Carolina admits that while the risk of primary cardiac arrest (i.e., sudden death from heart attack) is slightly increased during the hour or so of vigorous exercise we engage in each day, this is associated with an overall *decrease* once you factor in the days' remaining hours. Joggers are less likely to die of heart attacks, he suggests.

Dr. Siscovick identified only one death while running per 18,000 healthy men a year. Paul Thompson, M.D. of Miriam Hospital in Providence, Rhode Island found similar numbers in that state: 1 per 15,270. "That's a quite rare event," says Dr.Thompson, who adds that women almost never have problems, because of a lower incidence of coronary heart disease.

"Exercise is like investing in the stock market," says Dr.Thompson. "You're interested in long-term capital gain. If someone told you there was only a 1 in 15,000 risk of losing your investment in stocks, of course you'd do it."

As for whether running killed Jim Fixx, it was the immediate cause, but not the reason he suffered his heart attack. Ernst Jokl, M.D. of the University of Kentucky Medical School points out: "Exercise does not kill. A pre-existing disease does." The prime reason Fixx died young was genetics. His father had suffered a heart attack at age 35 and died at age 43. Fixx outlived his father by nine years. He might have lived even longer had not Fixx avoided obtaining a complete physical examination.

Eight months before his death, Fixx visited Dr. Cooper's Aerobics Center while researching a magazine article. Dr. Cooper offered to test Fixx's fitness. For whatever reason, Fixx demurred. A later autopsy showed 95, 85 and 50 per cent blockage in Fixx's three main arteries. Dr. Cooper believes that a stress test would have revealed this blockage. Various surgical techniques then could have been used to open the arteries, and Fixx still might be running today!

This underlines the necessity for people over 40–particularly those who exercise vigorously–to get regular physical examinations that include stress tests. This would include athletes who participate in world-class competition. The ability to complete a marathon is no longer believed to confer immunity from the illnesses that plague ordinary people as they age.

As one who both competes as a master and reports on the sport, the psychological as well as physiological benefits of masters competition seem obvious. One of my most rewarding recent activities was picking the annual All-

American team for *50 Plus*. In the seven years between 1981 and 1988 that that magazine presented its team, the publication nominated seven runners, as well as athletes in other sports who run as part of their training. With one exception, the seven began (or resumed) running late in life. This cast included Sister Marion Irvine, a nun who qualified for the Olympic Trials at age 54, and Clive Davies, a retired architect, who broke three hours for the marathon at age 69.

The team included Frank and Bill Havens, brothers from Harburton, Virginia and Manteo, North Carolina, who competed in Olympic canoeing when young. At the 1952 Olympics in Helsinki, Finland, Frank Havens won the 10,000 meter canoe race. Thirty-five years later in his 60s, he was capable of beating his gold medal time by a full minute. "That's the boat, not me," admits Havens modestly.

It included Margareta Lambert of Dillon, Colorado, also in her 60s, who wins national championships in downhill *and* cross country skiing during the winter, then switches to track (800 meters), race walking (1,500 meters) and cycling during the summer, winning all those events at the 1987 U.S. National Senior Olympics. "I'd like to try kayak racing," muses Lambert, "but I just can't find the time."

Irene Obera, a high school principal from Moraga, California, made the finals as a sprinter at the U.S. Olympic Trials in 1960 and the semifinals in 1968. Obera gave up running after that to pursue other sports, saying she "just got tired of it."

In 1974, Obera fell seriously ill with sarcoidosis, an inflammatory lung disease. She was bedridden for nearly a year, and while recovering heard about the first World Veterans' Championships in Toronto. Obera decided to give track and field another try.

In Toronto, Obera won two bronze medals–yet was disappointed. "I thought nobody could beat me," she says. Few have beaten her since. Between 1975 and 1989, Obera won more than two dozen medals at world masters meets, mostly gold including victories in the women's 100, 200 and 400 meter races at the 1985, 1987 and 1989 World Vets. Her times in the 200 and 400 for women 55-59 (W55) in Eugene were 28.48 and 66.99 seconds respectively, world W55 records. "My overall goal is to beat everyone in my age group in any event I am in," Obera says. She rarely fails. "Irene always is able to get ready for the big meets," says her coach, Enver Mehmedbasich.

Some of the most amazing masters athletes are those who compete in the upper age brackets. At the 1989 World Vets, Derek Turnbull, a farmer from Invercargill, New Zealand won six gold medals from 800 meters through the marathon in the M60 age group, placing second only in the 5000. Ed Benham of Ocean City, Maryland came close to matching Turnbull's total, winning five gold medals in M80, including a time of 45:20 in the 10 Km road race that would make most runners 50 years his junior happy. Benham is a former jockey, who began running after retiring in 1976 from his job as an outrider and equipment handler in the jockey room. "It's always a pleasure to run," he says.

Runners such as Obera, Turnbull and Benham seem to refute claims that running damages knees and joints. The feats of Frank and Bill Havens in canoeing and Margareta Lambert in her many sports similarly deny the dangers of masters sports. Some evidence suggests that running, and other aerobic exercises, may actually prevent (or relieve) the pains of arthritis by increasing circulation. The clinical picture is not yet clear. I can only offer as evidence my own body, which has 40 years of running wear. My knees sometimes ache at the start of a run, but not enough to stop me or slow me down. We are born biomechanically different. Some runners may suffer knee pains because of uneven strides. If shoe orthotics cannot cure the problem, they may need to switch to another sport.

Jack Greenwood refuses to switch, although he missed the 1987 World Vets in Melbourne for medical reasons. Greenwood of Aurora, Colorado, had won anywhere from two to seven gold medals in each of the previous World Veterans' Championships. A sprinter and hurdler, Greenwood had never lost a hurdle race in world competition, beginning in 1975. But the previous April, Greenwood, then 61, suffered a heart attack at work and needed bypass surgery.

No cardiac cripple, Greenwood is elated today because of how rapidly he recovered. "Doctors told me they could detect no heart damage," claims Greenwood. "All that running I did paid off. It didn't prevent my having a heart attack, but it enabled me to survive one." Greenwood followed a gentle walking program for eight months and resumed running in January. Soon, he was back competing in hurdle races. "I'm running as fast as before my attack," he says. In Eugene, Greenwood set world records while winning the M60 400 (57.64) and 300 hurdles (43.49) and also won the 110 hurdles (15.03). *National Masters News* editor Al Sheahen described Greenwood's victories as, "three of the most impressive performances of the meet."

To some, Greenwood's rapid return might be considered misplaced zeal. They fear he has forgotten how old he is. But isn't that the whole point of masters competition? In summary, senior sports is, indeed, safe. Although approaching your first starting line should not be done hastily, there is no reason why anyone can't begin to enjoy the benefits of masters athletics.

3. BASE FITNESS

Not everybody either has the talent nor the inclination to compete as a masters athlete, whether at the world level or even in local competitions. Five thousand competitors at the World Vets--or 3400 athletes over 55 at the Senior Olympics–seems impressive until you match those numbers against the 32 million Americans who jog, or the near equal numbers who exercise on stationary bikes, or walk for both enjoyment and good health. The masters movement, indeed, is merely the tip of a fitness iceberg that remains largely submerged.

Competition aside, most people who take up sports in their 20s and beyond are merely seeking base fitness–whether they identify it by that term or not. They seek answers to the following questions: How can they maintain a high fitness level on minimum training? What physical activities can they engage in to both feel good and reduce chances of heart attacks? Are there secrets to not merely getting in shape, but staying in shape? What is the *least* they can do and still remain fit?

Most exercise physiologists also would like answers to those questions. They would attempt to define base fitness. In his "Aerobics" approach, Dr. Cooper focuses on the body's ability to move oxygen-rich blood through the body. He stresses the cardiovascular-pulmonary system, which he considers paramount in determining quality of life. "This system must be maintained at an adequate state," he says.

To do so, Dr. Cooper assigns points to different aerobic activities, suggesting fitness can be maintained by scoring between 30 and 35 weekly aerobic points, which you can earn by running two miles in less than 20 minutes, four times a week. Different levels of swimming, cycling and other sports score similar points.

Ralph S. Paffenbarger, Jr., M.D., the Stanford physician whose studies of Harvard alumni convinced him that exercise *can* extend life, suggests calories burned as a measurement of base fitness. Burn 2000 calories a week through some fitness activity and you'll live better–and maybe longer–suggests Dr. Paffenbarger. To burn that many calories, you would need only jog or walk 15-20 miles.

Another index of base fitness is the American College of Sports Medicine guidelines mentioned in Chapter 1. Michael L. Pollock, Ph.D. of the division of cardiology at the University of Florida College of Medicine helped design them. The A.C.S.M. recommends 15-60 minutes of exercise, 3-5 days a week. "If you're talking *minimum* fitness," says Pollock, "I'd suggest a half hour three days a week."

Cooper, Paffenbarger, Pollock and other researchers come close to agreeing on what the average person, within general guidelines, must do to achieve, and maintain, base fitness. More tricky is the question of what any specific individual must do. Training is highly individualistic. What may be a routine workout for one person might detrain another.

Nevertheless, researchers finally have begun to consider questions centered around base fitness. At the University of Illinois at Chicago, Bob Hickson, Ph.D. organized experiments related to both training and reduced training. For ten weeks, groups of faculty and student volunteers at U.I.C. trained intensively under Hickson's direction: six days a week, 40 minutes a day. In each workout they pushed their heart rate to 90 to 100 per cent of maximum, alternating cycling and running to avoid injuries. At the end of a ten-week period each group showed improvements in fitness levels (maximum oxygen uptake) of 20 per cent. (Improvements of

15 to 25 per cent might be expected when relatively untrained people begin to exercise in a well organized program.)

Then over the next 15 weeks, Hickson *de*trained his subjects, focusing on three variables. With different groups, he reduced 1) duration (length of exercise), 2) frequency (how often), or 3) intensity (how hard). In examining duration, he cut their workout time to 26 or 13 minutes instead of 40. Looking at frequency, he had them exercise four or two days instead of six. In both instances, the subjects maintained close to their previously acquired fitness. Only when they worked at lesser intensity, did they begin to decline.

But does this mean that we all must run marathons or enter six-day bicycling events? If so, fitness may be an unattainable goal for the masses. Not everybody is equipped either physically or psychologically to train at high intensity, and obvious dangers exist. What about Pollock's identifying intensity as the one factor that drives people away from exercise. In one experiment Pollock used high-intensity interval training (sets of short, fast runs with walking in between) to obtain great improvements in fitness levels. But almost half the subjects dropped out of the program before its completion. "It wasn't much fun," Pollock admits. Experiments involving jogging or walking resulted in a higher participation rate. "With walking, almost everybody remained," says Pollock.

Is walking enough to keep us in shape without getting involved in masters competition? Probably so if we do enough of it and walk fast enough. The average person burns approximately 100 calories if they cover one mile on foot, whether they run that mile in five minutes or walk it in 40. That sounds unfair, but calories burned are calculated on the amount of energy required to move a certain mass across a certain distance. If we accept Dr. Paffenbarger's

2000 calories as our standard for base fitness, all you need do is walk around 20 miles a week, which could be accomplished in less than an hour a day.

Dr. Cooper, meanwhile, believes fitness can be measured by his simple point system based on aerobic exercise. At first glance, Dr. Cooper (with his 30 aerobic points) and Dr. Paffenbarger (with his 2000 calories) seem to disagree. If your exercise is jogging, you can please Dr. Cooper by running a minimum of eight miles a week at a gentle 10:00 per mile pace. That would score 36 aerobic points. Since each mile run burns approximately 100 calories, it seemingly would require 20 miles to please Dr. Paffenbarger.

But Dr. Cooper points out that Dr. Paffenbarger's study included even such background exercise as climbing stairs or walking to the bus stop in accumulating the weekly 2000 calories. "If you compare what he says with what I say," states Dr. Cooper,"my people scoring 35 points are probably burning at least 2000 calories." Marathon running and sweaty aerobic dance routines count, but so would mowing the lawn and having sexual intercourse. Although researchers quibble over points and calories and various other means of measuring fitness, they do agree on one thing: many methods can be used as ways to get fit and stay fit.

There's an important benefit that both doctors agree upon. "For each hour of physical activity, you can expect to live that hour over, and one or more to boot," says Dr. Paffenbarger. Dr. Cooper notes that one of the most dramatic findings of the Paffenbarger study was that exercise could expand the lifespan of a middle-aged person by two to two-and-a-half years. "That may not seem like much," says Dr. Cooper, "until you realize that if cancer were completely eradicated in this country, our lifespans would increase by exactly that same amount."

Sweating is necessary, Dr. Paffenbarger claims, but it does not matter how hard you sweat. "You do not need bursts of energy to add years to your life," he says. "There is no benefit from vigorous sports. You don't need to run marathons. Walking is enough." Dr. Paffenbarger found that if you burned more than 3,500 calories, it produced no additional benefits. The top line of Cooper's target zone was 80 points.

Work by Dr. Paffenbarger and others shows that moderate exercise can reduce the chance of heart attack by lowering blood pressure and increasing the protective cholesterol known as high-density lipoprotein, or H.D.L. It also helps the heart pump more blood with less effort.

Even as much a commitment as 35 aerobic points or 2000 calories may discourage many people, but Ronald LaPorte, Ph.D., an epidemiologist at the University of Pittsburgh, believes that base fitness might be achieved with even less effort. LaPorte reviewed the literature of studies related to cardiovascular heart disease and concluded that regular activities as mild as gardening and walking offered protection. "It's *activity* that's important," LaPorte stresses, "not necessarily exercise."

Another important factor could be what William P. Morgan, Ed.P., a psychologist at the University of Wisconsin refers to as, "the time-out effect." Go for an hour's bike ride and you leave behind the telephone and all your problems. Also not to be overlooked is the effect of diet on longevity, even though the relation of high cholesterol levels to heart attacks has been questioned lately. Research by John Holloszy, M.D. at Washington University in St. Louis showed that if you exercise rats they may not live longer, but at least they have a greater chance to attain their life expectancy. However, starve rats (feed them less food), and they will live longer, exceeding life expectancy. But is this fitness?

David L. Costill, Ph.D., director of the Human Performance Laboratory at Ball State University and a competitive masters swimmer, believes that fitness is more than avoiding heart attacks. Stay lean, don't smoke, and you'll probably live long whether or not you walk around the block. "What are we trying to accomplish with exercise?" asks Costill. "Are we trying to keep our arteries open, our muscles at a certain level of strength, our mental processes sharp, or do we simply want to visit fine restaurants after our workouts? You tell me why you're exercising, and I'll tell you how hard you're supposed to train, and how often."

Pollock believes that the cardiovascular-pulmonary system (the heart and lungs) is only one of the five major components of fitness. The other four components are body composition (lean or fat); muscular strength; muscular endurance; and flexibility. "They're equally important," insists Pollock.

But when everything is important, nothing is important. One of the problems in trying to get scientists to pinpoint base fitness is that if they fail to define it, they never will find it.

Those of us with lesser scientific backgrounds and reputations, whose quoted words and research papers are going to receive less scrutiny from our peers, have no trouble determining base fitness. We're fit when we know we're fit. When our bellies hang over our belts, when we wheeze walking up stairs, when our backs hurt after carrying the groceries, we know we're out of shape. Ask the average person to rate himself on a fitness scale of one to ten, and he won't need a treadmill test to get the answer. Despite impressive numbers of people joining the ranks of master athletes, we still are a nation of twos and threes.

Granted, how do we edge into the fours and fives? Although precise answers elude the scientists, finding base fitness is no secret to the average person. The typical American has been deluged the past decade with videotapes by the stars, how-to books by doctors, and articles in magazines. It's almost impossible to spend 24 hours in America without encountering some message related to getting in shape. The message is: a) get out and do something, and b) do it regularly, and c) keep doing it, and d) if you feel pretty good, you've probably found base fitness.

Let's consider some related questions.

What do you do? Jogging, cycling, swimming, walking, the activity doesn't seem to make much difference as long as it raises your heart rate, i.e., gets you breathing moderately hard. Dr. Cooper was pleasantly surprised to discover that after his patients injured themselves in one activity, say running, and switched to another, cycling, swimming, or rowing, it seemed to have little effect on their test scores. "A variety of aerobic activities can be used to maintain minimum fitness," Dr. Cooper advises.

How often do you do it? The A.C.S.M. guidelines suggest three to five days a week. "If you're talking minimum," says Pollock, "three days." Two days training a week provides some improvement, says Pollock, but not as much as three. The A.C.S.M. chose five as its top line, because studies show that people who exercise that often have a greater chance of injury, which may cause them to become discouraged and drop out of the program.

How hard do you go at it? Hickson's experiments identified intensity as an important factor in both attaining fitness quickly, and holding it. Many exercise leaders use target heart rate as one means to monitor exercise, having people raise their pulse to between 70 and 85 per cent of maximum. Most people, left alone, probably will reach that target naturally. Jack Wilmore, Ph.D. allowed subjects running on a treadmill at the University of Texas at Austin to set the controls to where they thought they were getting a good workout. "We measured heart rates and they were right on target," he says.

How much time do you take? The A.C.S.M. guidelines suggest 15 to 60 minutes. The wide variation reflects the fact that some people can train intensively over a short period of time and burn as many calories as others whose approach is more leisurely. That does not suggest that either has the right or wrong approach. The consensus among most exercise physiologists is that 30 minutes is about right. "One of the reasons why people drop out is lack of time," says Pollock.

How long will it take? Most people who begin fitness programs begin to feel good once they get past the sore-muscle and fatigue phase. That usually lasts one to three weeks. "Within a month you probably reach a significant level of improvement," says Costill. "It's very measurable at that point." After two or three months, people working at a steady rate reach a plateau, the point we have described as base fitness.

How much more can I improve? Gains beyond your base fitness point will be more difficult to realize. A person can improve their aerobic capacity by 20 per cent within two to three months. Three months more work of increasingly difficult training might result in only a few more percentage points of improvement, if that. The fitter you are, the tougher it is to improve. That's the Catch-22 of fitness.

How soon will I lose it? This relates to the half-life of fitness, just as Uranium has a half-life by which it decays. Scientists hedge their answers when asked this question, because research is scanty and inconclusive. Most believe you go out of shape as fast as you got into shape. The best controlled studies have been done by Edward F. Coyle, Ph.D. at the University of Texas at Austin. Coyle found that within 12 to 21 days, a group of runners lost half their aerobic fitness. After another 12 to 21 days, they lost another half–and so on. By three months, all were detrained. Such conclusions frighten many lifetime fitness freaks and masters athletes. They fear that if they relax for an instant, they also risk losing their hard-gained conditioning. Twenty years of train-ing can go down the tubes in three months. "The body has no memory of how continuously you have trained," warns Costill.

Base fitness, once found, thus can easily be lost. So once you achieve it, don't let go.

4. BEGINNINGS

With a city the size of New York, what are the chances that someone from the Midwest could walk down Broadway and meet another Midwesterner? Surprisingly, it happens to me all the time when I visit New York on business. Recently, I encountered Ed Winrow, a former national champion road runner, whom I first met when he was studying for a masters degree in the 1960s under Dave Costill at Ball State University. Later, he coached at Valparaiso University. I sometimes trained with Ed and his team. I still have on my kitchen wall an abstract painting by his wife Rita.

Winrow moved east to coach at Mansfield State University. The next time I saw Ed was in the late 1970s when my son Kevin was competing in the N.C.A.A. cross country championships in Pennsylvania. Ed had gained 60 pounds and was smoking cigars. The descent of the mighty, I thought.

But when I saw Ed during the summer of 1988, he had just accepted a new job as fitness director for the New York Athletic Club. If not back to his former size and shape, at least he was close–and he had abandoned those awful cigars. Disgusted at his own slide, Winrow had resolved one day to get back in shape. "The first day out the door was toughest," he admitted. "After that, it was just good to be back, regardless of how slow I was running." Winrow had not returned to competition, but was thinking about it.

What happens to the body of a man or woman past the age of 40 when they start to train again for competition? The mind may remember what it took to get in shape when young, but maybe the body isn't ready for that level of stress–and may never be again. The memories of games played, and races run earlier in life, can be a trap.

Complicating matters are the effects of aging: it is easier to train as an athlete in your 20s or 30s than in your 40s and 50s. Beyond 60, some scientists suggest walking may be all the aerobic exercise we need–or should take. Also a factor is how long you have been away: someone maintaining a fitness base by jogging a few miles every other day will return easier than someone who quits for several decades. And someone who *never* competed in sports while young must explore new ground.

Never having competed is not all that unusual for masters athletes, particularly women for whom there was little competitive activity (other than cheerleading) when they were younger several decades ago. During the 1989 World Veterans' Championships, I appeared at a sports medicine conference with Joan Ullyot, M.D., author of "Women's Running."

Dr. Ullyot, who has run marathons under 3:00 in her 50s, described how she once sat on the sidelines when younger and watched men compete. Sometimes she didn't even do that. While attending Wellesley University, famous among runners for being the halfway point of the Boston Marathon, Dr. Ullyot never came out of the dorm to watch marathoners pass. Years later, she found herself running the same race past her alma mater.

Many masters athletes may have competed in one sport while young, only to try a new activity later. Record setter Ed Benham raced for many decades–but always atop horses. He was a jockey. Only after retirement, did Benham turn to competitive running. Someone whose only youthful sporting experience was baseball, indeed, begins anew when he contemplates, at the age of 39, his first marathon.

One problem is that as people age, they exercise less. According to a 1985 Gallup Poll, commissioned by *American Health*, 54 per cent of adults surveyed claimed they exercised regularly.[1] But as people get older, the percentage declines. Among those age 18-29, 66 per cent said they "work out." Among those over 50, the percentage is 41. Most distressing, 10 per cent of non-exercisers use the excuse, "Too old."

Kenneth H. Cooper, M.D. vigorously refutes that idea. Dr. Cooper once told me that, while exercise cannot *halt* the aging process, he is sure it can *slow* aging–and slow it considerably. "By improving your physical fitness, you'll look and feel much younger than your calendar age," adds Dr. Cooper.

Nevertheless, even seemingly fit individuals find they must rethink their approach to exercise when they decide to enter the competitive world that exists beyond fitness. What tips can we offer masters athletes in their quest for a higher level of conditioning?

While scientists have succeeded in measuring the effects of detraining (how quickly we go out of shape), they find it more difficult to measure *re*training (how long it takes to get *back* in shape). "There's very little data," concedes Michael L. Pollock, Ph.D., director of the Center for Exercise Science at the University of Florida. Nevertheless, we can make some educated guesses. Edward F. Coyle, Ph.D. of the University of Texas at Austin suggests that every week lost requires two weeks spent in recovery. David L. Costill, Ph.D., director of the Human Performance Laboratory at Ball State University estimates that you can regain aerobic fitness within four to eight weeks. "Strength changes take longer," he adds.

----
1. Even this percentage seems unrealistically high. To many Americans, exercising means going to the beach and sitting in the sun with a beer can in one hand.

People with previous conditioning return to shape faster than people starting from scratch. In other words, a born-again runner has an advantage over one who never started. "The muscles may have some memory," muses Costill, "or maybe we're smarter with our training the second time." Ball State's William Fink adds: "A lot depends on how far you've gotten out of shape. There comes a point where you've lost everything, when starting over means truly starting from scratch."

Fink, a confessed slow runner, lost more than a year of training due to a knee injury caused when he attempted to move a TV set. After surgery, Fink resumed jogging and, within a few weeks, found himself able to run five miles. "It seemed it took me longer to reach that level when I first started 20 years ago," he says. Fink had done some cycling during his sedentary year and believes that allowed him to maintain some base conditioning. He adds: "Runners are notorious for thinking they're out of shape even if they've laid off only two days."

The very best athletes, however, find it most difficult to regain past peaks. Part of the problem is motivational. For those who have won the gold medal–or even come close–anything else they achieve might seem an anti-climax. Only a few Olympians continue in competition through their master years. One exception is Al Oerter, a four-time gold medalist in the discus who has continued throwing competitively into his 50s–although, admittedly, more often in open competition than against his age peers.

Oerter believes the effect of age in weight throwing to be minimal, though admitting that he has lowered his goals. "I can train as long and as often and with as much intensity," he says, "but athletics is still just my hobby. I enjoy the goal-setting, the hard work, the feeling of testing myself against folks of a similar mind. But I don't feel I have to win or live up to someone else's expectations."

Few top athletes stay active as long as Oerter. They recognize the amount of effort it requires to reach the top–or stay there. They become unwilling to pay the price. Or they may be unable to because of accumulated injuries. If they have allowed several years of little or no training to pass since their peak years, they may fear the effort required to regain lost glory. They may not want to get beat by former rivals who train harder as masters. When you're at the elite level, improvements of a few seconds require herculean efforts involving months, maybe years, of hard training. At that level, you can't afford time off; it's too difficult to climb the mountain again. Alberto Salazar and Dick Beardsley ran one-two in record time at the 1982 Boston Marathon. Both, soon after, were plagued by injuries, and although Salazar and Beardsley continue to run for enjoyment, neither have quite regained their lost glory.

Coincidentally, I encountered both within a short period of time during the summer of 1989. While in Eugene for the World Vets, I saw Salazar at a party given by orthopedist Stan James. "I'm training harder than ever," Alberto confided in me, hinting a return to competition some time soon. Later that week at a banquet for the vets, Salazar announced that he looked forward to turning 40 in nine years.

Alberto was probably just being polite, but several weeks after that, I saw Beardsley at a 10 Km in Shabbona, Illinois. Dick was there as a celebrity rather than competitor, but it was obvious that he retained his love for running. "I'd like to get back to my former level," Beardsley told me, "but something always gets in the way." Sadly, several months later Beardsley severely mangled one leg in a farm accident, threatening his ability ever to run again.

One part of me says I would enjoy seeing Alberto and Dick hammering at each other the way they did at Boston in 1982. Another part says, is it really that important for my or their future happiness? Probably not. Less inclined to get philosophical about such matters are new joggers whose only goal is to feel good again, not win the Boston Marathon. A few miles more, a few calories less, some other simple lifestyle adjustments, can result in mammoth fitness gains.

In Coyle's detraining studies, he identified one reason for the immediate fitness decline as loss of blood volume. During the first 12-21 days away from training, you lose as much as half a quart (500 ml) of blood. Coyle claims: "Previously, researchers thought detraining was because of deterioration of the heart. Actually, the heart had less blood to pump to the muscles."

When you *re*train, you regain that lost blood volume. Not only can you now transport oxygen to the muscles more efficiently, but you have more fluid available for sweating, which helps cool your body. For this reason, you are better off starting training during the cool days of spring rather than waiting for summer when your body may not be acclimatized to the heat. Coyle claims runners can regain blood plasma volume (fluid) fairly rapidly, within a week, although reproduction of lost red blood cells takes longer.

Not all training benefits vanish during long layoffs. Fast-twitch muscles hold some of their endurance. Muscle capillaries, which increase by 40-50 per cent in training, remain and retain their ability to eliminate the waste products of exercise, such as lactic acid. But not all systems of the body detrain or retrain equally. Your skeletal system, for instance, may not accept the strain of training at your previous level, particularly as you age. A runner who loses six years of training, as did Ed Winrow, mentioned in the lead of this chapter, must also cope with six years of normal aging. Many people who take up sports as masters have done little training in recent decades. Some never have participated in sport more organized than a touch football game in grade school.

There is also the problem of extra weight, the excess body fat that sedentary people accept as part of the normal human condition. Even assuming that all other physical parameters were equal, a person weighing an extra 25 pounds could not run, or swim, or cycle as fast as his previously slim self. If you don't believe so, try doing those activities with a 25-pound pack on your back. One problem with gained weight is that the body adapts to the excess and may resist a return to what the reborn athlete considers his best fighting weight.

Beginning at age 25, the average American adds 1.5 pounds of body fat per year. This gain of fat may not be entirely reflected in the person's gain in total weight, since some of the fat gain is balanced by loss of lean body mass (muscle and bone).

This fattening of Americans continues until about age 55–an average gain of 45 pounds body fat. At this point, standard weight curves begin to show a decline in weight. This statistical decline, however, may be in part because larger people begin to die, claims Jack H. Wilmore, Ph.D. of the University of Texas at Austin. "The fattening actually continues," says Wilmore. "The weight of those surviving into their late 50s may plateau, but they still add fat in place of lean body mass."

As we age, we also lose muscle. With the decline in muscle comes a decline in strength, most noticeable among people past 60. As muscles atrophy, the result is a shriveling effect, that makes us look, as well as feel, older.

Masters athletes retain muscle better than sedentary individuals–although certain muscles deteriorate sooner than others. Fast twitch muscle fibers (those associated with strength) atrophy first, slow twitch fibers (those associated with endurance) later. After age 30, muscle fibers decrease at a rate of 3 to 5 per cent each decade. This can result in a loss of up to 30 per cent of muscle power by age 60. Simultaneously, there is a progressive loss of the motor nerves that connect the central nervous system to the muscles. The total decline may be linked to the aging body's inability to retain protein. Aging becomes a form of gradual muscle dystrophy.

The fibers you lose are the ones you use the least. In normal, daily activity, the fibers you use most are slow twitch, so you retain those. The fibers used least are fast twitch.

So to maintain muscle strength, it becomes a case of "use it or lose it." By continuing to use both forms of muscle fiber, masters athletes can retain those fibers longer–though not entirely halt the loss. Trained athletes also are more successful at recruiting a higher percentage of available fibers, not only during exercise, but also during regular activities. Even though a certain amount of muscle loss is inevitable, you can maintain general strength by better utilizing the muscles remaining.

Can masters sports help you retain muscle strength? Sure, but there are limits. Running, for example, exercises mostly the lower body. Among masters runners, the upper body may still lose muscle mass, as much as four pounds a decade according to studies of runners by Pollock.

Cyclists exercise the lower body; swimmers exercise the upper body. Among the so-called aerobic sports, cross country skiing comes closest to providing so-called "total fitness," exercising the entire body. Racewalking with its vigorous arm-swinging also is a good total exercise. So is rowing, if done properly, pushing off with your legs. Athletes in sports that rely on only upper- or lower-body muscles should add some strength training, such as light weights, for the lesser used muscles. "You need a well-rounded program," warns Pollock, "because if you don't use the entire body, it will deteriorate and eventually affect your overall fitness."

Another factor in the aging process is the weakening of bones, most common among sedentary people. Those who exercise maintain more bone strength. Runners thus suffer less from osteoporosis, a degenerative disease that weakens bones and results in 700,000 fractures a year, mostly hip. It is a disease that affects older women, but men are not immune–assuming they live into their 80s. And whether or not you suffer from osteoporosis, everyone suffers from bone loss as they age.

Drinking milk and (for women) estrogen supplementation can help limit bone loss, but physical exercise is equally important. "There's no doubt that exercise is beneficial to the bones," says Barbara L. Drinkwater, Ph.D. of Pacific Medical Center and a past president of the American College of Sports Medicine. Another factor is that those who exercise maintain muscle strength and coordination. "Active people will suffer fewer falls, plus they'll be able to protect themselves in a fall," says Drinkwater.

Still another symptom of aging is a decline of work capacity, identifiable in the laboratory through downward changes in the volume of oxygen consumed per minute during all-out effort, the so-called "VO_2 max" that has become the bellwether measurement of fitness. Among sedentary individuals, this decline occurs at an approximate rate of 1 per cent per year after age 25, partly a result of lost muscle, as above. Since muscles consume most of the oxygen during exercise, any reduction in muscle mass reduces maximal oxygen consumption.

Other factors affecting capacity, according to Everett L. Smith, director of the Biogerontology Laboratory in the University of Wisconsin's department of preventative medicine, include the capability of the heart and lungs. But though aging causes a definite loss of work capacity, sedentary individuals can regain much of what they lose. Smith states, "It is possible to regain up to 50 percent of the loss of cardiovascular function with regular exercise."

Those of us who never stop competing do even better. For two decades, I have been one of a group of two dozen masters runners studied by the University of Florida's Michael L. Pollock. Pollock began measuring us at the National Amateur Athletic Union (now T.A.C.) Masters Track & Field Championships in San Diego in the summer of 1971. That was my first experience as a masters athlete; I had just turned 40 only a few weeks before the meet. In a race that Peter Mundle and I remember well, I barely outkicked him on the home stretch of the 10,000 meters. (That was back when masters competition was in 10-year age groupings, and Peter was giving away several years to me.)

In the period since 1971, Pollock has brought the two dozen originally tested back into the laboratory at regular periods. He notes that our decline in work capacity is only half that of sedentary people. The group declined 5 per cent a decade, or half a percent a year. Among those who continued to train at the same intensity, there was virtually no decline. "Inevitably those runners must slow down too," Pollock has written. "We can only tolerate high intensity training for so long. But their physical fitness and overall youthfulness will remain much higher than others their age who do not run or participate in equivalent activities."

I make no claims for myself, but research at Harvard University by Phillip Whitten and Elizabeth J. Whiteside suggests that those who exercise regularly also have more active sex lives. Among 160 masters swimmers studied, 97 per cent aged 40-49 claimed to be sexually active; 92 per cent in the 60-69 age group per cent said the same. Whitten and Whiteside reported this as quite high compared to the sex lives of the general population older than 40. (Alfred Kinsey previously had documented declines with age.) The masters swimmers reported intercourse seven times a month, a frequency similar to people in their 20s and 30s. Swimmers in their 60s proved nearly as active sexually as swimmers in their 40s.

It's enough to make all of us want to plunge into the pool.

Not everyone, however, should plunge into masters sports without undergoing a long and gradual retraining process. If, having reached the age of 40, you desire a return to competition, here are some tips to get you started:

1. Start slowly. In fact, start *very* slowly. Unless you were a track athlete while younger—and maybe not even then—don't rush out the door and start running hard on your first day as a masters athlete. Begin by walking. Take several weeks, or months, to develop a base of physical fitness before you even consider doing anything that resembles "training." This is particularly important if you are overweight.

A good opening workout, regardless of your sport, would be to exercise in some manner, easily, for 15 minutes. Walk, jog, cycle or swim, but keep it simple. Work up a good sweat, but not *too* good a sweat. Particularly for the first several weeks, ignore the temptation to measure how far you've gone, or how fast you got there. Stopwatches and tape measures are best avoided during your early stages of training, because they can easily discourage you—or cause you to push too hard too soon. As you make the move from fitness athlete to masters athlete, you will have ample time for measurement, both against yourself and, in competition, against others.

2. Obtain a complete physical examination that includes a stress test. That's good advice whether or not you exercise, particularly for those over 40. It's also a good idea to continue to obtain physical examinations on a regular basis, at least once every second year, more often as you get older. A stress test involving walking or jogging on a treadmill, or pedaling on an exercise bicycle, is a safe but effective means of detecting cardiovascular problems. Such exams can detect other problems, such as cancer from which exercise provides little immunity.

Most modern hospitals now have cardiovascular departments capable of performing stress tests. Most cardiologists are knowledgeable in administering those tests. And most insurance companies have awakened to the advantages of preventative medicine, reimbursing clients who take tests. There is really no excuse any more not to get a full check-up.

3. *Watch your weight.* One of the standard measurements of fitness is maximum oxygen uptake, usually expressed in a number that signifies the liters of oxygen consumed per minute per kilogram of body weight. Regardless of your ability to consume oxygen, you score better if you weigh less. You'll also perform better if you weigh less—at least to a point. Therefore, it behooves each masters athlete to attain his or her ideal competitive body weight.

This usually is best determined over a period of time by seeing at what weight you do perform well. (Too little weight and your performances may deteriorate.) One of the best ways to lose weight is steady aerobic training. Every mile run, biked or swum equals so many calories burned. This is the reason why body-builders hop on exercise bikes after their weight-lifting stints: to reduce fat for better muscle definition.

Another way to lose weight is to pay attention to diet, specifically how much you eat. Don't think you need to go on a starvation diet to get in shape, but by combining a well-balanced diet with regular training, you most easily can attain your best competitive weight.

4. *Seek advice and companionship.* One way to motivate yourself is to join a class or a sports club. By training with others, you not only will enjoy the social environment, you can push yourself more to excel. To improve technique in a skill sport, you may want to take lessons. Summer camps once were only for Boy Scouts, but masters athletes

now attend camp to learn how to be better runners, cyclists, swimmers and triathletes. Don't overlook the advice you can get in books or magazines and on videotapes.

5. *Forget the past.* Workouts done years ago bear no relevance to what you can do today–and can be a cause of injury if you try to duplicate them without your past level of fitness. Once you regain your base fitness, you can ask yourself whether you want to (or can) resume old training patterns.

Can you do it better? In your previous life as an athlete, did you make mistakes that can be avoided this time around? Reevaluate your entire approach to training. Don't get trapped in old training habits that maybe didn't produce best results.

6. *Sore muscles are part of the price you may pay.* Accept that fact. Any time you push your body, it may rebel and tell you it hurts. Some pain is part of the natural process of strengthening muscles. But too much is bad. Back off and go easy. Give yourself one or two days rest between sessions.

Don't undervalue easy workouts. For someone untrained, a half mile seems as tough as a marathon. Learn to appreciate slow runs at short distances. There will be time for hard workouts after you regain your aerobic base.

Consider your age. Runners in their 20s bounce back after layoffs as though they never had quit. It becomes progressively difficult to regain, and maintain, lost fitness once into your 30s, 40s, 50s and beyond. But not impossible. Use techniques such as stretching and creative rest that you might have ignored while young.

7. *Have a goal in mind.* At first, your goal may be as simple as going out to train the first day. Ask yourself why do you want to exercise again: To get in shape? To compete in some race? Plan your training well ahead so as to achieve that goal.

Many masters athletes exult in competition, particularly national and world championships. They find that top-flight competition forces them to excel and gives them both an excuse and a reward for all their hard training over the years. Others are happy to compete only on the local level–or not at all. Both approaches to fitness are correct. Whatever level of participation you choose, you can motivate yourself better by selecting some specific goal, even one so simple as losing the five pounds you gained over the holidays.

8. Be regular. Don't train hard for a period of time, then quit before beginning again. Fitness is a lifetime commitment. You don't need to train every day, but you need to train regularly to maintain your level of conditioning. Even if you decide to back away from competition for whatever reason (burnout or injury), don't stop exercising entirely. The A.C.S.M.'s recommended 15-60 minutes of exercise, three to four days a week, is a relatively easily attained level for anybody interested in maintaining the positive benefits of fitness. If you maintain your training at this minimal level, you will find it easier to get back in shape if your competitive desire returns.

9. Wear proper equipment. The most (perhaps only) essential piece of equipment for runners is a good pair of running shoes. Avoid discount shoes that only look like running shoes, but don't offer proper cushioning or fit. Swimmers usually find training more comfortable if they use noseplugs and goggles, but can get by with only a bathing suit. Cyclists and skiers, on the other hand, can literally spend thousands of dollars to equip themselves properly. Every athlete can benefit from comfortable (and fashionable) clothing.

Regardless of your sport, obtain equipment that can help you both maximize performance and prevent injury. (As a sometime cyclist, I would not consider mounting my bike without donning a protective helmet. That its aerodynamics also help me bike faster is another plus.)

10. Don't overdo it. Some intensity is necessary to attain peak performance. But until you rebuild your aerobic base, too intense workouts may cause excessive fatigue and discourage you. Even with that base, your tendons and ligaments may not support the power developed by your lungs and muscles.

Remember also that just as strength is slowest to fade when you stop training, it takes longest to return. Strength equals speed. You will find it toughest to regain the top end of your conditioning, even when back in reasonably good shape.

Also, don't race too soon or too often. Competition can be a good way to measure your level of fitness, but you risk injury by going too hard. Enter competition with a relaxed mood, and you'll enjoy it more.

5. IMPROVING WITH AGE

Early in 1987, a New Zealand farmer named Derek Turnbull, who started running at age 13 and never quit, traveled to Australia to compete in the City of Adelaide Festival Marathon. The day was cool and Turnbull proved well prepared. He crossed the finish line in an all-time personal record best of 2:38:46.

Turnbull was 60 at the time!

"Nobody else over 60 had broken 2:40 before," commented Turnbull, so I thought I would give it a go." Later during the year, the Kiwi won six gold medals at the World Veterans' Championships in Melbourne.

Few athletes in any sport can continue to improve as they approach 60. Yet Turnbull might be considered only semi-unique. Alex Ratelle, M.D., an anesthesiologist from Edina, Minnesota, won the state mile championship in high school, but failed to compete in college. After racing sports cars during his 20s and 30s, Ratelle returned to running in his 40s and 50s, establishing his best-ever marathon time of 2:31:56 in 1978 at age 53. Appropriately, Ratelle made his mark at Grandma's Marathon in Duluth, Minnesota.

Ratelle, now in his 60s and still setting age-group records, does not regret his postponed athletic career. "I especially enjoy running at this time in my life," he says. "Imagine the thrill of going out and scaring younger runners to death."

Norm Green, a minister from Wayne, Pennsylvania, ran the mile in 4:24 while attending the University of California at Berkeley. Green did little running for 15 years while establishing a career with the American Baptist National Ministries and raising a family of four. Eventually, he started running again, but trained 13 years without seeing the necessity of entering an organized race. Lured to the starting line of a San Francisco fun run by his brother at age 49, Green rekindled his lost desire for competition. Several months later, Green finished his first marathon in 2:35:51. In 1984 at age 52, Norm Green improved to a remarkable 2:25:51.

Can masters athletes continue to improve with age? The experiences of Turnbull, Ratelle and Green would seem to suggest an affirmative response to that question. But endurance seems easiest to maintain. It is more difficult for aging athletes to demonstrate improvement in speed events, such as the 100 meter dash, or skill events, such as the pole vault. Eventually we all slow down. That fact is evident when you compare the winning performances at any masters competition, regardless of sport. With the exception of occasional super-athletes, the times are greater, the distances and heights lower, as you go from young to old.

As example, take the 100 meter dash results–men and women in five-year age groups–from the 1989 World Vets. Here are the winners:

35	(not contested)		Jacqueline Apayou	12.65
40	Eddie Hart	10.87	Phil Raschker	12.57
45	Thaddeus Bell	11.49	Silke Mattelson	13.03
50	Ken Dennis	11.48	Wendy Ey	13.66
55	Ron Taylor	11.89	Irene Obera	13.93
60	Peter Mirkes	12.36	Shirley Peterson	14.57
65	Ewald Kleinmann	13.52	Paula Schneiderhan	15.11
70	Payton Jordan	13.28	Anna Binder	18.74
75	Yuichi Tateishi	15.30	Johanna Gelbrich	18.46
80	Harry Gathercole	15.63	Bertha Hielscher	20.93
85	Charles Booth	16.98	(no entrants)	
90	Ching-Chang Wang	23.15	(no entrants)	

With the exception of a few remarkable individuals–Dennis and Jordan among the men, Raschker and Gelbrich among the women–the times of the 100 winners get progressively slower relative to age. The same is true in other track and field events and in other sports with the performances of women usually trailing those of men by several age groupings.

This decline is inevitable and hardly a surprise to anybody. It is the reason why masters compete in age groups. Not only is the decline statistically predictable, but it also is the basis for a series of age-graded tables, which are sometimes used for handicapping competition.[2] At the end of the 1989 T.A.C. National Championships, a 100 meter dash with cash prizes placed Herb Anderson, winner earlier of the M85 division, 27 meters in front of the starting line with other champions also offered age-graded handicaps related to their ages. Payton Jordan, M70, caught Anderson and Harry Gathercole, M80, but in the final stride got passed by Bill Collins, M35, and Ken Dennis, M50. "I'll get them next time," vowed Jordan. Collins won $250; Dennis, $150; Jordan, $100. The winners in a similar women's race were: Irene Obera, W55; Una Gore, W50; and Margaret Girouard, W45.

Yet despite the inevitable, *average* decline of athletic performance experienced in all masters sports, *individual* athletes often continue to improve for many years. This is particularly true for those who take up a new sport in middle age. When you start as a novice, every movement is upward. Jack H. Scaff, Jr., M.D., the cardiologist who founded the Honolulu Marathon and organizes the highly successful Honolulu Marathon Clinic that trains people to

----
2. Developed by W.A.V.A. and *National Masters News* with the help of many individuals throughout the world, the 66 page "Masters Age-Graded Tables" are available for $5.95 plus $1.30 postage from: *N.M.N.*, P.O. Box 2372, Van Nuys, CA 91404.

finish that race, believes that a person who begins running at age 40 can continue to improve for 13 years with intelligent training.

Improvement is only difficult for those who have participated in a specific sport for a long time–and even they can continue to get better if they gradually elevate the quantity and/or quality of their training. (In some sports, improved equipment results in improved performance.) When all else fails, you always can switch sports. A runner who becomes a triathlete not only can improve as a triathlete, but can also chart improvement in cycling and swimming. (This was a major reason for the initial success of this sport, populated originally by runners who probably had topped-out with their 10 Km and marathon times, thus needed new motivational goals.)

William Andberg, M.D., who in his late 70s continues to practice as a veterinarian in Anoka, Minnesota, was a three-time intercollegiate snowshoe champion in college and also ran cross country. After a three-decade hiatus, Andberg resumed running and soon became one of the top masters runners in the world. He has won so many World Vets gold medals at distances from 800 to 10,000 meters, that he professes not to know the number. In 1983 at the world nordic skiing masters championships, Andberg won four gold medals. He has held as many as 28 different records at one time in masters track. Andberg also was national seniors champ in bowling in 1983 and has as one goal rolling a 300 in bowling to go with a recent hole-in-one in golf. (His bowling average: 172.).

Andberg's secret: "Whenever I start a new sport, I take lessons." But there are different ways by which masters can continue to improve. Here are a few:

1. *Do more.* The simplest formula for improvement–used by the young as well as the old–is to continue to increase the *quantity* of your training. Sports scientists refer to this as the principle of "overload." Do

more and you get better. The ancient Greeks recognized the overload principle while training for the Olympic Games. One Greek legend relates the tale of Milos. To strengthen himself for wrestling competition, Milos began by lifting a young calf overhead. As the calf grew in size and weight, Milos continued to lift him daily, growing in strength. Soon, the calf had grown into a large bull with Milos still hoisting him overhead. Milos possessed such strength that none of his opponents could defeat him.

People who prepare for a marathon follow the training principal pioneered by Milos. First, they jog a mile. Several weeks later, they're up to two or three. Soon, they find they can run comfortably for a half dozen miles, and maybe they enter a 10 Km race to test themselves in competition. Eventually, their appetite is whetted to follow the footsteps of Pheidippedes, the legendary messenger who carried news of the Greek victory in the Battle of Marathon to Athens. (Supposedly, Pheidippides died after shouting, "Rejoice we conquer!" but that's another story.)

Over a period of months, these embryo marathoners gradually increase their weekly mileage and the distance of their longest training runs. Typically, marathoners try to build to the point where they can comfortably run 20 miles at one time. Then they go into the race, counting on inspiration to carry them the extra 6 miles 385 yards. Usually this does occur, and they cross the finish line triumphant, having scored an important personal victory. Even novice runners realize that if you want to succeed, you first increase the quantity of your training.

This is true for swimmers too. As a senior at the University of Ohio at Athens, David L. Costill swam on a relay team that placed third at the National A.A.U. Championships. After college, with a doctorate in physiology, Costill taught at Cortland State (New York) University and coached cross country and swimming. Aiming to lose weight and break 6:00 for the mile, he began jogging. Eventually he ran 5:28 and developed into a good middle-of-the-pack marathoner while turning the Human Performance Laboratory at Ball State University into one of the top sports labs in the world. At age 47, Costill resumed his career as a swimmer, first swimming for exercise, then entering some local masters events at the urging of friends. Early success spurred him to increase his training load.

Costill soon found himself swimming faster than his collegiate times. He hit his peak at age 51 when he won 13 national titles in masters competition. Costill's time in the 200 individual medley at that age was 2:23, compared to his best of 2:16 at age 21. Costill attributes this success primarily to increased yardage: "Back in college, the most I did was 1,500 yards a day, but as a master I would do that much just in warm-up."

2. *Do it faster.* As athletes continue to train more, there comes a time when improvement ceases. Even Milos found he no longer could increase his workload at the point when the bull overhead stopped growing. Although some runners run 140 miles or more a week, and swimmers and cyclists cover equivalent distances in the pool or on the road, sooner or later the body rebels at increased workloads. The athlete is forced to go slower and slower while going further and further. Chronic fatigue sets in, a phenomenon called "overtraining."

If the body fails to rebel, the mind may. Many busy people find it impractical to train much more than an hour a day. On the other hand, I have heard a number of masters athletes approaching 65 express the thought that retirement from work will finally allow them more time to devote to training. They become, at the end of their careers, full-time jocks.

But for continued improvement, most athletes find they must add speedwork. Costill concedes that while his initial improvement came when he increased yardage, he soon after also added speed training. Rather than doing more, athletes do it faster. Instead of improving the *quantity* of their training, they improve its *quality*. The simplest way to increase speed is to stabilize the distance you cover and try to run that distance faster each day. For instance, a runner might improve his training pace of 8:00 per mile to 7:30 to 7:00 to 6:30 and so forth. A weightlifter would cease trying to lift continuously heavier weights, but would keep the weight the same and try to hoist it more often. Or the lifter would shift to lighter weights, but more repetitions.

Runners who do speedwork often run quarter-miles on the track. They run one lap at top speed, then rest by jogging or walking before doing another. A typical speed workout by a middle distance runner would be 10 x 400 meters near race pace, jogging 400 meters between. This is called "interval" training, because runners control the speed of their rest laps (the interval between sprinting) as carefully as that of their fast laps. Or, when the focus is mostly on the fast laps, the workout may be referred to as doing "repeats." The runner will run hard, then relax until ready to go again. A typical workout of repeats might be 3 x 400 at full speed with maximum rest between. An infinite variety of training plans are possible depending on, a) how you vary the distance you run, b) how fast you run the distance, and c) how much you rest during each interval, or between each repeat.

Swimmers practice a similar form of training, typically sprinting a length (or lap) of the pool, then holding onto the gutter before sprinting another length. Because of the nature of their sport (less pounding), swimmers typically can sprint closer to their top speed and need less rest between laps. They also can log large numbers of repeats. It's not unusual for a top swimmer to do as many as 50 50-meter sprints with as little as 10 seconds rest between.

Cyclists who do similar speedwork call it "jumps." Cruising along at a steady pace, they suddenly jump out of the saddle and pedal at top speed for a brief period of time. During a workout of several hours, covering as much as 40-

50 miles, a top cyclist might suddenly do a dozen such jumps to break the pace. Cyclists often utilize handlebar computers that can be set to beep at regular intervals, say every 60 seconds. They pedal hard for 60 seconds, easy for 60, hard for 60 again, and so on. The computers also count pedal revolutions per minute and speed as well as distance and time covered. Using a computer to vary speed can help convert an otherwise monotonous ride into a form of play. Experienced cyclists often look down on such devices as unnecessary, but they can be a godsend for novices trying to improve.

A less structured form of speedwork favored by runners is *fartlek*, a Swedish term meaning literally "speedplay." Normally, runners do fartlek in the woods, or on soft surfaces such as a golf course. In a single workout, they do bursts of speed varying pace, distance and rest, responding to signals from their bodies rather than a handlebar computer: picking out a tree and sprinting to it, then resting until recovered before picking out another tree. It is a freeform style of training requiring experience to perform properly.

3. *Get stronger.* Most athletes use weight training as an adjunct to their regular training. A strong muscle can push harder and faster, so strength equals speed. The advantages of weight training is obvious in strength events, such as the shot put and discus throw where competitors typically are big and muscular. Jumpers and sprinters also can improve their spring and speed by getting stronger. Distance runners need more endurance than strength, but may benefit from a general strengthening program that involves high repetitions of low weights.

Can pumping iron make you a better athlete? That's a tough question, and it depends partly upon your sport. Gabe Mirkin, M.D., author of "The Sportsmedicine Book," once wrote about lifting in *The Runner.* "There is no proof that (lifting) will in any way improve your times," claimed

Dr. Mirkin. I don't disagree with Gabe. Frequently at running clinics I tell people, "I'm not sure lifting works unless you're running short distances." Then I'll proceed to demonstrate the weight exercises I use.

Following Dr. Mirkin's comment, a reader from New Jersey wrote: "Dr. Mirkin may be correct for runners blessed with a fair amount of upper-body strength. But I had very little strength to begin with and have found (after six months of Nautilus training) that I can now run any race without the extreme fatigue I formerly felt in my shoulders and arms." Good point, yet if weightlifting results in excessive upper-body bulk, sheer weight will slow you. Masters athletes, particularly runners, also need to be cautious of lower-body exercises (particularly squats or leg lifts with heavy weights) that might weaken, rather than strengthen, knee joints.

Nautilus has a different machine for each muscle group. The theory is that you exercise each muscle to exhaustion, lifting as much weight as you can so that you still get eight to 12 reps. When you reach 12, you increase the weight next time and try for eight. It's the 20th century equivalent of Milos and his calf.

Whether or not weight lifting will improve your times or distances, it will allow you to develop (and maintain) a higher level of overall fitness. During the long-range study by Florida's Michael L. Pollock, Ph.D. on the aging of a dozen masters runners, including myself, he brought us back in 1983 and compared our fitness levels with that of a dozen years before. Eleven no longer competed, and they showed more decline than the 13 who still did. And of that 13, there were only three who had shown little or no decline in a decade. I was one of this Gang of Three. What we had in common was that we all engaged in some form of weightlifting. That might be good enough reason to continue pumping iron.

4. *Get a coach.* Perhaps the surest way toward improvement–yet one of the most difficult to achieve for masters athletes–is to find some knowledgeable individual to supervise your training. A few masters athletes train under the supervision of coaches; Irene Obera comes to mind. When Peter Mundle was at peak performance setting records in his 40s, he trained under the supervision of Joe Douglas at the Santa Monica Track Club. In New York, Bob Glover provides coaching-for-a-fee for members of the New York Road Runners Club and other clients. But the great majority of us are self-coached, gaining what insights we can on training from publications such as *Runner's World* and books like this.

The American system works remarkably well to develop young athletes. The age-group opportunities for grade-schoolers is hit-and-miss, depending on where you live, but most high schools have reasonably well developed programs in cross country and track and field. Recently, I began coaching my local high school cross country team, boys and girls. Most of the other coaches in our area (many of them runners themselves in their spare time) were very competent and good at motivating their charges. I learned much from them. Even if a talented athlete fails to receive good coaching while in high school, he often can pick his coach at the next level. Despite cut-backs in recent years, the American collegiate system has provided an excellent proving ground for Olympic medalists.

Beyond that point the system breaks down. Unless an athlete demonstrates Olympic potential–and sometimes not even then–he or she will find coaches few and far between. In Europe, where competition in the schools is limited or nonexistent, sport clubs provide coaching for their members. But in the U.S., most running clubs operate differently. They organize road races and social events, but provide little coaching, particularly for sprinters, jumpers or weightmen who need it the most. A masters athlete who decides to take up the javelin late in life has a real problem.

No easy solution exists for masters seeking coaches. One possibility is to connect yourself to an existing program at your local high school or college. Most coaches at that level can use help, even if it is only holding a stop watch or picking places at a track meet. You help them and they may help you.

Another method is to seek help from your fellow competitors. Once the medals have been decided but before they are awarded and everybody goes home, most athletes enjoy talking among themselves and are free with tips and advice. Don't be afraid to ask questions, even of competitors who finish behind you whose knowledge may be greater than their ability. Young athletes, particularly distance runners, often attend summer camps to fine-tune their skills. More such camps, particularly the Florida Runners Camp, organized by Atlanta's Roy Benson, have begun to encourage masters to attend.

In obtaining masters coaches, we need to help each other. If you belong to a running club, particularly a large one with financial resources, lobby for the addition of coaching services to the club program. As the masters movement continues to grow, coaching may become more and more available. It's one area where we need improvement to improve.

Improving the basics of endurance, speed and strength will guarantee improvement almost regardless of your sport. Masters athletes also can get better by improving their technique and equipment. Running involves such elementary movements that some experts believe that technique comes naturally, that it either cannot or should not be taught. "People run as they do because they have to," Fred

Wilt, former women's coach at Purdue University, once said. "They don't have any choice. A lot of time is spent coaching things you don't have to, and this is one of them."

Swimming, however, is much more the technical sport, one that requires much attention to proper form in the several strokes in which swimmers compete. In bicycling, having good (and often expensive) equipment becomes almost as important as having strong legs to push that equipment, but an experienced cyclist who knows both how to tune that bike and how to position himself on it, and shift properly, will outrun novice cyclists on the most expensive machines. When you combine swimming, cycling and running, the triathlon offers almost infinite opportunities for improvement, which is one of that sport's appeal to masters athletes who may have seen their performances turn downward in their regular events.

Even accepting Wilt's statement, a few things can be said about improving running form:

1. *Footstrike.* Most better runners land on their mid-foot, that is, at a point just behind the ball of the foot. They then drop down on their heel, their bodies rotating across a foot that is planted firmly on the ground, before pushing off with the toes. Some run more forward on the ball (toe runners) and others land more flat-footed (heel runners). The worst form fault in footstrike is to try and adjust your landing to accommodate what you think other runners do.

2. *Stride length.* There is no perfect stride length, only perfect stride lengths (plural) for individuals depending on their individual characteristics. In long distance races, however, a short, quick-tempo stride may waste less energy than a long stride that causes the runner to lose momentum by pushing too far ahead of his center of gravity. But under-striding can be as great a sin as overstriding.

3. *Carriage.* The trunk should be more or less perpendicular to the ground and the hips forward. The Finns say you run from the hips, and American Olympian Garry

Bjorklund once told me: "Novice runners have a tendency to sit down, to put their weight behind them. They need to bring their center of gravity forward and get their weight over their metatarsals."

4. *Arm carry.* Arms should swing in rhythm to the legs, forward more than sideways, with hands cupped rather than clenched. Bill Bowerman, track coach at Oregon, liked to have his runners carry their arms high across the chest. Jumbo Elliott of Villanova wanted his runners to carry their arms low, "thumbs in their pockets." If two great coaches such as those can differ as to what is proper form, there may be no proper form.

5. *Head position.* The head serves as keystone for the rest of the body. Back in some paleolithic era, a coach once told me to fix my gaze 10 yards up the track and use my eyes to anchor my head in a relaxed position. That is probably as good advice as any. If you allow your eyes, and gaze, to wander all over the road, you probably will wander with them.

6. TRAINING SMART

After the end of the 1985 World Veterans' Championships
in Rome's Olympic stadium, I caught a bus from the
Cavalieri Hilton Hotel to Leonardo da Vinci airport and
found myself sitting next to Paul Spangler, M.D. A retired
surgeon, Paul had won four gold medals at the Games.

We had not met before, but knew who each other
was. Dr. Spangler then was 86 and at that upper age level,
you often collect medals just by appearing to declare yourself alive. But Paul is a genuine competitor, who has set
dozens of records since he began running at age 67 out of
concern for his health. "My records will be broken," Paul
told me. "The kids keep getting faster." (By "kids," he
meant runners in their 60s and 70s!)

Like most in masters competition, Dr. Spangler displayed a vigor equal to that of people decades younger. It is
partly physical fitness that provides youthfulness for the very
old. More than that, it is the sense of purpose that comes
with competition in masters sports. Dr. Spangler possessed
with many other athletes over 40 a shared goal. "I've got
friends all over the world," he remarked.

As we chatted amiably, the bus passed a field of
sunflowers. Dr. Spangler briefly interrupted our conversation to alert others on the bus to the beauty around. Our
ability to continue enjoying such beauty motivates many of
us to pursue our various goals in masters sports.

"My ambition is to run until I'm 100," Paul told me.
"The way I feel now, that should be easy."

Athletes like Dr. Spangler survive partly because experience teaches them how best to train their bodies. We
get smarter. During a period of peak performance between

1972 and 1975, when I was between 41 and 44 years old, I ran a time for 10,000 meters that was within two seconds of my all-time best and a time for the 3000 meter steeplechase that was only four seconds off my bests in 1956 at age 25. My 5000 time missed by only 16 seconds my best effort from my youth. I also ran several road bests at 15 and 30 Km that probably approached performances from a decade or two earlier when course measurement was much less precise. And at age 49, I ran a marathon at the 1981 World Vets in a time that, while eight minutes slower than my personal record, still was faster than any of about a hundred others I had run during a long lifetime of running. Moreover, the 1981 effort was on a hot day when others were running three or four minutes slower than their recent bests.

It doesn't figure. Everything I know about sports science tells me that I should *not* have been able to maintain that level of performance into my fifth decade. But during those decades, I had accumulated a level of knowledge about training my body that permitted me to come closer to maximizing my potential. I suspect that most other masters athletes you see with medals hung around their necks at the various championship meets have done the same. We've learned to train smart.

What can we learn from these masters? As a fitness reporter, I have had the opportunity to interview many other athletes and pick their brains for training tips. Following are ten ways by which you may be able to maximize your performances:

1. *Learn from the best.* The principles of technique and training are the same for all runners, regardless of ability. If you want to improve, you need to follow the same training patterns as the elite. Particularly in skill events, technique remains the same regardless of age. Watch other runners and see how they run. Ask how they train. Most athletes are eager to share their ideas, even with competitors who might some day beat them.

2. *Develop your own pattern.* The same elite train at a level that would destroy most masters. Even if you were able to match an elite athlete in a single workout, you probably would not be able to do so day after day without self-destructing. You want to learn from top athletes–regardless of your event–but not follow them blindly. Everybody has different levels of abilities and limits to those abilities. How can you modify the training patterns of the elite to fit your own particular skills and limitations?

3. *Find your red line.* Each athlete has a point in training where he self-destructs. Some runners thrive on 100 miles a week, whereas others become injured going past 30. Sometimes by training yourself very, *very* carefully you may be able to gradually edge your red line to a higher level, allowing yourself to compete also at a higher level. But push too far and you risk injury or the flatness that comes from overtraining.

4. *Listen to your body.* It's the biggest cliche' in fitness sports, but one worth heeding. The aches and pains that come after (and during) exercise are messages telling you it's time to slow down, back off, rest before pushing forward again. Body messages are the most important signals as to how your training is progressing. You ignore them at your own risk.

5. *Keep track of your training.* The best way to learn from your successes and failures is to keep a training diary. If you set a personal record in your event, was it because you practiced twice as hard the month before, or because you did almost nothing after a hard previous month? You'll never know unless you record your workouts and competition. Most distance runners keep diaries that include how far and how fast they run each day plus weather and track conditions. Athletes in other sports can benefit from similar record-keeping.

6. *Don't be trapped by your diaries.* Just because you once ran a dozen 400 meter sprints under 70 seconds doesn't mean you can do it again. For one thing, you may be 10 years older. If you improved your training during those 10 years, you actually may be able to run faster, despite a decade of aging. In most cases, you will want to modify and improve your training (which may mean doing less) based on past experience.

7. *Rest is as important as hard work.* Most top athletes follow the hard/easy pattern pioneered by retired University of Oregon coach Bill Bowerman. They train hard one day and rest the next so they can train hard again the third. Costill of Ball State claims muscles gain in strength only when rested. Two to three hard days of training a week are plenty for most masters athletes.

8. *Spare your body.* Many top masters runners do much of their training on grass, dirt trails, or rubberized tracks. They avoid, when possible, hard surfaces. Soft-surface running may be the key you need to avoid injury. Pay attention, also, to your footwear. A worn-down pair of heels, or an old pair of shoes that has lost its compressibility, may be a possible cause of injuries.

9. *Change training patterns gradually.* If you don't, you may discover that your body rebels. If you're already in good shape, you may push yourself into an injury if you change suddenly from long runs to speed work, or vice versa. A runner who tries skiing or a swimmer who starts cycling uses different muscles. While running on trails or grass may provide long-range protection, novice road runners often dislike uneven surfaces, fearing they may turn an ankle or twist a knee. Make your training moves gradually, giving your muscles time to adapt to the new stresses.

10. *Be wary of Father Time.* Many masters runners wisely eschew stopwatches. Runners who focus only on time do themselves an injustice, because the inevitable aging process that causes even great masters to slow from year to

year. Comparing this year's time, whether in training or races, with last year's becomes a downer. An athlete who attempts to match previous workouts on the watch is doomed to inevitable disappointment and, more to the point, risks overtraining resulting in injury. By taking the emphasis off the clock, masters focus on their present, rather than past, achievements.

7. SECRETS OF THE MASTERS

In 1987, I attended the World Veterans' Championships in Melbourne, Australia with notebook as well as running spikes. I was writing an article on masters training for *Runner's World*, eventually to be published in that publication's August 1988 issue. After my own competition, I talked with some of the top competitors, those who had won multiple gold medals, to see what insights I could glean on the art of success.

I spoke with New Zealand's Derek Turnbull, winner of six M60 gold medals in those Championships. I chatted also with Antonio Villanueva of Mexico, who won the M45 5000 and 10,000, then placed a close second in the 3000 meter steeplechase despite having aggravated a tendon injury during a fall in the water jump. Other multiple winners in Melbourne interviewed by me included: Jacqueline Hansen of the U.S. (W35), Irene Obera of the U.S. (W50), Derek Wood of Great Britain (M55), John Gilmour of Australia (M65) and Ed Benham of the U.S. (M80). Then there was Sweden's Kjell-Erik Stahl (M40), who won the World Vets' marathon by a half-mile margin in 2:21:38, then doubled back the following weekend to place in the top ten at the Honolulu Marathon.

What are the secrets of these masters who dominated their age groups in Melbourne? What can ordinary runners learn from these world beaters? Following is how they train.

1.   "ENJOY TRAINING"

Name: DEREK TURNBULL
Home: Invercargill, New Zealand
Born: December 5, 1926
Occupation: Farmer
Achievement: Won every flat event from 800 meters through the marathon in the M60 age group at the VII World Veterans' Championships. Earlier in 1987, Turnbull set his all-time personal best time of 2:38:46 at the City of Adelaide (Australia) Festival Marathon. "Nobody else over 60 had broken 2:40 before," says Turnbull, "so I thought I would give it a go."

Career: Turnbull began running in 1939 at age 13 and has competed continuously since. "I've run with one club all my life," he says. "For years, there was no vets' competition, but I enjoyed running weekends with the boys." The first World Vets occurred in Toronto in 1975. Turnbull failed to attend, but looked at the results and thought, "I can do better than that." He appeared at the second Championships in Gothenburg, Sweden two years later to win at 1500 meters. His Vets' medal count following the 1989 Championships in Eugene stood at 23 gold and three silver.

Training: "Fitness is half in your mind," says Derek Turnbull. "If you enjoy training, you get results." He claims to eat like a horse, sleep like a dog, and train "when and if I can with no stopwatch, no coach and no special diet."

Turnbull credits his basic strength to the rugged life he leads as owner of a 600-acre farm with 60 breed cows and several thousand ewes: "I'm on my feet all day, lifting, pushing. I never stretch or lift weights. It comes natural."

His training is simple: "I get a long run on Sunday with the boys, a fast-medium run middle of the week, and fiddle around in between." Sometimes returning from chores, he will jump out of the truck two miles from home

and run the remaining distance. Turnbull's long run sometimes stretches to 25 miles. "If I'm running through the bush
and climb a hill I've never seen before, that's a bonus."
Advice: "Never give up."

2.   "I'M RUNNING EVERY DAY"

Name: JOHN GILMOUR
Home: Leeming, Australia
Born: May 3, 1919
Occupation: Retired gardener
Achievement: Gilmour won the M65 10,000 meters
and cross-country at the World Vets, placing second at 1500
and 5000 to Australia's Jack Ryan, another world beater.
Earlier in 1987, Gilmour ran 15 Km in 55:33, placing in the
top 20 at the West Australian national championships, but
an ear infection following a virus caused him to miss two
months of training. "It affected my balance," Gilmour explains. "I tried to come back too fast running on a treadmill,
hanging onto the bars, and suffered a string of injuries.
Career: Gilmour started running in 1937 at age 18,
then "got buggered with the war." He spent three-and-a-half
years in a Japanese prisoner of war camp, but resumed
training after returning home, soon winning the Western
Australia 10 Mile Championships. Gilmour's time in 1946
was 62 minutes. In 1987, at age 68, he ran that same distance in 58 minutes.
   Gilmour was present at the beginning of the masters
movement, winning the 50-plus 10,000 and 5000 at the National A.A.U. masters track and field championships in San
Diego, California in 1971. He has competed in every World
Veterans' Championships, starting in 1975, winning a total
of two dozen gold medals at events from 800 meters to the
marathon.

Training: "Consistency is the secret," claims Gilmour. "I'm out running every day, summer or winter, regardless of the weather. You have to do the training if you expect success."

Claiming not to be blessed with extraordinary speed, Gilmour focuses his training on twice-weekly, interval, speed sessions. The first session, done usually on Tuesdays, is 16 x 500 meters, jogging 500 meters between. The second session on Thursdays, is 10 x 1000 meters, also with 500 meters jog rest. For long runs, Gilmour goes 10-15 miles.

Most older runners would self-destruct on such a regimen, but the key to Gilmour's success is not timing himself. "I never work on a watch," says Gilmour. "I run myself to my limit for that particular day. Runners who focus only on time do themselves an injustice."

Gilmour sometimes goes to the track, but more often runs his 500 or 1000 meter interval sessions on grass in a park near his Leeming home. "Even when I train for a marathon, I run on the grass," says Gilmour.

Advice: "Burning out is all in your mind."

3.   "AVOID RUNNING ROADS"

Name: J. DEREK WOOD
Home: Enfield, England
Born: February 18, 1931
Occupation: Retired bank manager

Achievement: Won cross-country and the marathon (2:40:30) in the M55 age group at the 1987 World Vets, also placing second in the 5000. Earlier in 1987 at the world road running championships (I.G.A.L.), Wood won three titles in three days: cross-country, 10 Km and 25 Km.

Career: Wood started running in 1949 after suffering several soccer injuries. He won a number of county championships, was named an alternate to one of Britain's international teams after placing fifth in the A.A.A. championships, and felt he was on the brink of joining the top ranks. Then, running the 3000 meter steeplechase, he landed badly in the water jump and tore ligaments in his foot. "After that, I could never get enough mileage in and eventually had to let it go," says Wood.

He stayed fit, nevertheless, while serving in the British Territorial Army, helped as a running club administrator after discharge, and continued to jog. "In my late 40s, I seemed to be running well," says Wood," so some of the guys in my club nudged me back into competition."

After turning 50 in 1981, Wood increased his training, winning British veterans' titles from 5000 meters to the marathon. He set a personal record of 2:33:20 at age 51 at the New York City Marathon.

Training: While working as a domestic branch manager for Barkley's Bank, Wood ran twice daily: three-and-a-half miles in the morning on a nearby cricket grounds and a similar workout in the evening. Weekends, he sometimes ran one race Saturday, another Sunday.

Now retired, Wood has abandoned his twice-daily schedule in favor of a single run of 8-12 miles, usually late morning. "I generally run steady with fartlek as it seems appropriate," he explains. (Fartlek is a form of training that involves bursts of speed, punctuated by slower running between.)

Wood avoids running on roads. "There's a lot of countryside near where I live, and I can run on paths through the forest, up and down hills. I'll put on a burst and sometimes push, depending on how I feel each day." Even when training for a marathon, Wood rarely runs longer than 12 miles. Before winning the marathon in Melbourne, his longest single run was 18, and that only once three weeks before the race.

Advice: "Every run is a bonus. Just to be taking part in sports is a great opportunity."

4.   "BLEND SPEED AND DISTANCE"

Name: KJELL-ERIK STAHL
Home: Ahus, Sweden
Born: February 17, 1946
Occupation: Telecommunication general manager
Achievement: Winner of the overall and M40 marathon titles at the 1987 World Vets in an unpressed 2:21:38, Stahl headed home via Hawaii and placed in the top ten at the Honolulu Marathon the following weekend: 2:31:07 for seventh. Earlier in the fall, Stahl won $1,500 for being first masters finisher at the Bank One Columbus Marathon (2:20:03) and $8,000 for a similar win at the Twin Cities Marathon (2:18:01).

Career: A soccer player when young, Stahl entered running as an orienteer, the sport that combines running through the woods with map-reading. A member of the Swedish national team between 1971 and 1976, he was Europe's top-ranked orienteer in 1973. A some-time track competitor during this period, he ran his first marathon in September, 1979, placing third (behind two Finns) in the Swedish national championships with a time of 2:16:49. In 1986, Stahl placed ninth in the European Championships with 2:13:14. His personal best is 2:10:38, fourth at the World Track & Field Championships in Helsinki in 1983, when he was age 37. His fastest time as a master is 2:12:33 in winning the 1986 Stockholm Marathon. It is second only to Jack Foster's record 2:11:19.

Training: A workaholic both in business and sport, Stahl spends 60 hours a week in his manager's job with Televerket in Kristianstad, Sweden and still fits in 80 miles training. "I've never done much high-mileage training," claims Stahl. "I race too much." Indeed, through the end of 1987 the tall (6 feet 4 inches, 168 pounds) Swede had run 70 marathons, 57 of them under 2:20.

Key to his training is a favorite 19-mile, forest trail, a20-minute drive from Stahl's home. Snow-covered during the winter, he usually begins training on it when the weather warms in March. "The trail has 12 major hills on it," explains Stahl. "I'll run it at least once every ten days, usually at a very hard pace."

Until recently, Stahl ran twice daily, but admits to have lost some of his earlier motivation, particularly when it comes to rolling out the door early into the dark and cold of a Swedish winter. "It's much pleasanter to run during the middle of the day when it's warmer," he says. "I'll try to do two workouts a day on weekends." Stahl's weekend routine consists of nine miles in the morning, 11-13 in the evening, both days. Or he may substitute his 19-mile run one day, usually Saturday, because he finds it hard to sleep after that hard a run. "It's almost like a marathon in that my body works so hard," he says.

To check conditioning, Stahl runs an interval workout on a bicycle path, seven to ten repeats of 1000 meters during a run of 12-13 miles. He carefully times each repeat, wearing two stopwatches to do so. Stahl believes his success comes from blending speed and distance: mixing interval training with weekly long runs, also fitting short races between his many marathons. "People wanting to improve know what kind of work to do," says Stahl. "They need to follow the same training schedules as the elite."

Advice: You must do some of everything. You can't always jog.

5.	"LEARN FROM OTHER RUNNERS"

Name:	ANTONIO VILLANUEVA
Home:	Jalapa, Mexico
Born:	July 25, 1940

Occupation: Physical education teacher and taxicab fleet owner

Achievement: At the World Veteran Games, Villanueva won the 10,000 and 5000, running 14:44.18 in the latter race despite rain, wind and cold weather, a performance considered by many to be the outstanding one by a distance athlete in the meet. Later, in the 3000 meter steeplechase, Villanueva was bumped and fell in the first water jump, injuring tendons in one leg. Forced to land flat-footed and lose 10 yards in each of the remaining water jumps, he still finished a close second in that event.

Career: Villanueva began running in the army at age 19 after a drill instructor sought to punish him by making him run around the track. Unable to compete in the 1968 Olympics in Mexico because of an injury, Villanueva broke his country's national record in the 3,000 meter steeplechase two years later, eventually improving his best time to 8:36.

Early in 1972, he beat Olympic gold medalists Gaston Roelants and Mohammed Gamoudi in a 5000 meter race in Czechoslovakia, but shin splits slowed him during that year's Olympics, and he failed to advance from his trial heat. Retiring several years later, Villanueva resumed serious competition just before turning 40. In 1982 at the Nike/OTC Marathon in Eugene, Oregon, Villanueva, age 42, ran 2:13:41.

Training: Villanueva feels his injuries when younger were caused by training on hard surfaces. "When I got off the roads and started training on dirt trails, I got much fewer injuries," he says. His favorite course is a five-mile loop on soft surfaces near his home. He runs each morning at 7:30 with a group from his club, including his son Hector. He adds a second workout later in the day.

Villanueva believes that age has given him a greater depth and maturity to understand and learn from the training of other runners. "I've learned from many runners, but I don't train exactly like any of them." One difference in

Villanueva's speed training is that he begins with short sprints of 200 meters meters and, over a period of months, progresses to longer ones of 1000 to 1600 meters. He describes this as *trabajo de corazon*, literally "heart work," designed to improve his aerobic capacity.

Advice: Just be consistent and stay healthy. Villanueva laughs when he offers this advice, adding: "I'm the one always getting injured, because I train too hard."

6.   "FOCUS ON AN EVENT"

Name: JACQUELINE HANSEN
Home: Topanga, California
Born: November 20, 1948
Occupation: Athletics consultant
Achievement: Though at the top of her W35 age class, Hansen won both the 1500 and 5000 meters at the 1987 World Vets. Her times were 4:42.21 and 17:43.09, the latter in atrocious weather. Hansen, however, was unconcerned about times, saying: "I just went for the wins. Both were tactical races, and I felt I ran two of the smartest races in my life." Hansen was returning to competition following a long layoff due to bunion surgery and felt she peaked exactly at the right time.

Career: Hansen began running in 1966, participating at Granada Hills High School in the first track and field class for women offered in the Los Angeles city school system. While attending San Fernando Valley State (now Cal State Norridge), she began training under Laszlo Tabori, although he coached at another college. Though qualified for the 1972 Olympic Trials at 800 meters with a time of 2:13, she didn't participate, feeling she was not fast enough to make the team. "I now regret not at least participating," says Hansen.

In 1972, Hansen ran her first marathon in Culver City, California, winning in 3:15. In 1973, she won the Boston Marathon in 3:06:26 and also the collegiate mile championship. Two world records followed: 2:43:54 at Culver City in 1974, and 2:38:19 at Eugene in 1975. She married masters runner Tom Sturak and gave birth to a son, Michael, in 1980. That plus a series of injuries caused Hansen to put her running career on "hold" until 1987.

Training: Rehabilitating, Hansen conditioned herself slowly: combining weightlifting and water-running (she teaches aqua aerobics) with easy distance running. "I intend to continue to train the same, even though not coming off an injury," she says. "The water made me supple and weights made me strong." In March, she began speed work, two days a week on a dirt track under the supervision of Tabori.

Hansen feels that following a structured program leading toward specific goals will help her prevent past injuries. She ran no marathons in 1988. "Trying to be a road runner year round got me into trouble," says Hansen. "I was more successful when I had a track season, a cross country season, and still had a rest season between." Her favorite workouts are running trails in the hills near her home in Topanga. She uses that for her distance base, later sticks to flat running on grass or a dirt track.

Advice: Figure out your best event and focus on it. That plus being consistent in training are the two keys to success.

7.   "RUN WITHIN YOURSELF"

Name: IRENE OBERA
Home: Fremont, California
Born: December 7, 1933
Occupation: High school principal

Achievement: Obera dominated the sprint events at the 1987 World Vets, winning the 100, 200 and 400 meter dashes, repeating her triple victories at the Games in Rome two years before. (In 1989, Obera again won the same triple.) In Melbourne, Obera also ran on the winning 4 x 400 relay team and the 4 x 100 team that placed second.

Career: Obera competed in basketball, field hockey and softball through college. The year after graduating in 1957 from Chico State University, Obera attended a track meet one day and said, "I could do that." Someone overheard and handed her an entry blank for a meet several months later. Challenged, Obera entered and won the 100 meters. During a decade of competition, she made the finals at the U.S. Olympic Trials in 1960 and 1968 (but not the team), then retired from running–she thought.

In 1974, Obera fell ill for nearly a year with sarcoidosis, a debilitating disease. Regaining strength, she learned about the first world masters meet in Toronto in 1975 and decided to enter. Disappointed at only winning two bronze medals in the 100 and long jump, she began training harder and now owns a dozen world championship gold medals, more than any other sprinter. She has never been beaten in the sprints by an American in her age group.

Training: Obera runs only three days a week, usually at a track, but does weight training with exercise machines two other days. "My strength is not what it was when younger," admits Obera, "so I have to supplement it or go down hill." At the end of each track season, she takes one or two months off, then begins a gradual conditioning program with mostly slow jogging, up to two or three miles.

During the competitive season, she focuses her training on 400 meters. "That's my toughest event," Obera explains. "If I can run 400, I can run anything below." Typically, Obera does repeats of 500's (endurance) on one day of the week, 300's (pace) another day, then 50 meter starts out of blocks (speed) the third day. She warms up thoroughly before each session, jogging and bounding, but gives equal attention to her cool down, saving her stretching for after her workout. "I'll do 20 minutes of stretching after I run and another 20-30 minutes later at home," says Obera. To avoid injury, she never wears spikes except in competition.

Advice: Run within yourself, not straining. Also, everything I do is geared for me. People should learn from other runners, but not necessarily copy them.

8.   "DON'T JUST SCRUFF ALONG"

Name: ED BENHAM
Home: Ocean City, Maryland
Born: July 12, 1907
Occupation: Retired jockey
Achievement: Including team competition in cross-country, Benham won six gold medals in Melbourne. He scored on a M70 team, but his individual wins came in M80: 800, 1500, 5000, 10,000 and cross-country. In the upper age groups, competition can be spotty, but Benham demonstrated by his times in the 1500 (6:04.26) and 10,000 (45:49.27) that he knows how to run fast. Earlier in the season, he ran a world age-group best of 3:43:27 at the Twin Cities Marathon.

Career: Weighing only 66 pounds, Benham rode his first race as a jockey in Culver City, California in 1923 at age 14; his first victory came two years later. During a career that lasted until 1940, the 5-foot-4 Benham's riding weight was 110 pounds. He still weighs 112. Benham remained at the track until 1976 as an outrider and equipment handler in the jockey room.

Soon after retiring, he began doing some running with his two sons, who previously had participated in track. "The first time I raced," recalls Benham, "I won a $50 certificate, and that got me hooked." His second race was the

Nike Cherry Blossom 10 mile in which he set a new age group record. Benham has continued to set records, nearly 100 American road and track records.

Training: Benham believes in simple training, doing a regular 50-60 miles a week along the ocean, mostly on the road, but sometimes on the packed beach. "It's always a pleasure to run," he says, "although I'm not too good on speedwork." He claims that he trains himself like he once helped train horses: "I go out at a steady pace for a few days, then if I'm feeling good, I open it up a bit." Typically, Benham runs 3-4 miles in the morning, has breakfast, reads the paper at breakfast, then if he feels he needs more miles to maintain his regular schedule, goes out again in the afternoon. His normal pace is about 7:30 to 8:00 per mile, not too far from his race pace.

"When I'm in good shape, I'll push myself," he says, "although not all the way. I'll sprint out in the middle of a run, and that's the only kind of speedwork I do." Benham attributes his lack of injuries to the fact that he avoids speedwork. He adds: "One thing I'll say, I do my training faithfully. And I don't go out there and just scruff along."

Advice: "If your body tells you to back off, do it!"

In summary, what can we learn from these remarkable masters? Sweden's Kjell-Erik Stahl claimed that the principles of training were the same for all runners, regardless of ability. Stahl advised: "Follow the same training schedules as the elite."

By this, Stahl meant not copying his routine of 19-mile trail runs and 1000-meter speed sessions, but rather copying the *pattern*. Most top masters I interviewed at the World Vets in Melbourne followed a similar pattern, one characterized well by Derek Turnbull: "I get a long run on Sunday with the boys, a fast-medium run middle of the week, and fiddle around in between."

Sound advice, Derek. With variations, the same formula probably works for masters sprinters, jumpers and throwers as well. That's the ultimate secret of the masters.

8. MAINTAINING MOBILITY

The dormitory elevator at San Diego State University moved sullenly downward. Crammed with competitors from the 1989 U.S. T.A.C. National Masters Track & Field Championships, it seemed to hold forever on the sixth floor. Impatient, an Australian punched the "Close Door" button–then quickly apologized. "Just using the button to save a few seconds," he said.

"I wish I had that kind of button for my legs," grumbled a British runner.

Who wouldn't want a magic button to hold back the ravages of time? That masters may be aging more gracefully than those who never exercise is beside the point. You can't deny the stop watch that tells us, indeed, we're slowing down.

Part of the problem is diminished mobility. We're tighter, we're stiffer, and as a result, we don't run as fast–or recover as quickly. Despite the lack of a magic button, masters can maintain better mobility through a combination of muscle-loosening techniques that include stretching and massage. After winning the 5000 meters in San Diego mid-morning, I hurried to the dormitory, pausing at a Seven-Eleven store to purchase a 75-cent bag of ice. Sitting on the root of a tree, I positioned the ice bag under the calves of my legs, tight after the hard run, then hopped on a table for a pre-scheduled massage from therapist Rose Tripoli. A warm shower, some easy stretching and several hours in bed with my legs raised completed the process. That afternoon, I was back on the track for the finals of the 1500 meters.

Did the combination of ice, massage, stretching, heat and rest allow me to recover more rapidly? It's hard to say. In the finals, Jim Sutton of Pennsylvania and Chuck Wemberley of New Mexico left me in the dust, although I was able to out sprint the others on the final straightaway for a bronze medal.

Whether or not a magic button exists for maintaining mobility, stretching and massage do help. Let us consider these two important techniques:

STRETCHING

Recently, I volunteered to coach the high school cross country team in Michigan City, partly for enjoyment, partly for conditioning, partly to test some training theories. Heading out on a long run one afternoon, I stopped the team after about a mile to stretch in a park. I noticed that Don Pearce, a senior, was just standing there, not stretching. When I asked him why, Don replied, "I don't have any flexibility."

"Of course," I said. "Because you never stretch."

Ironically, Don was my fastest runner, having qualified for the state championships the previous spring at 800 meters with a 1:57. But despite possessing good speed, Don often looked tight in races. I felt that if I could get him to loosen up, maybe he could run still faster.

Everybody–young or old–can benefit from a loose approach to their sport. Flexibility training, or stretching, has become increasingly important for athletes trying to maintain mobility. Bob Anderson, author of "Stretching,"[3] perhaps the most popular book on the subject, points to

---

3. Available spiral-bound for $10.95 plus shipping from Bob Anderson, P.O. Box 767, Palmer Lakes, CO 80133; (800) 333-1307. Anderson also sells a video tape, which will get you loose for $29.95 plus shipping.

pitcher Nolan Ryan as an example of a flexible athlete. When Anderson was teaching flexibility drills to the California Angels, Ryan was one of his most apt pupils.

"Ryan was a very limber person," Anderson recalls. "He could virtually do the splits. When you consider what a pitcher must do when he throws the ball, you realize that the action requires a great deal of flexibility. If you measured most hurlers in certain body positions while they threw, you would find they were extremely flexible."

Anderson considers stretching important for various reasons. First, it reduces muscle tension and makes the body feel more relaxed. Stretching also helps coordination by allowing for freer and easier movement. It can also increase range of motion and promote circulation. Finally, stretching makes you feel good.

Marybeth Brown, Ph.D., assistant professor in physical therapy at Washington University believes that flexibility actually includes two components: range plus strength. "If you can raise your arms 180 degrees, fine, but next comes the question, how fast can you go through that range of motion? Strength and flexibility are inextricably related to one another. Obviously the stronger you are, the more capable you are of getting through your entire range of motion, and actually adding to your mobility."

"Stretching also helps prevent injuries such as muscle strains," claims Anderson. "Activities become easier, because you are prepared to perform. Stretching signals the muscles that they are about to be used." Anderson considers stretching to be an important link between the sedentary and the active life. "It keeps the muscles supple, prepares you for movement, and helps you make the daily transition from inactivity to vigorous activity without undue strain," he says. "Stretching is especially important if you run, cycle, play tennis or engage in other strenuous exercises, because activities like these promote tightness and inflexibility. Stretching before and after you work out will keep you flexible and help prevent common injuries."

Stretching is particularly crucial for masters athletes, who tend to lose flexibility with age. Our joints literally "dry up," causing an inevitable loss of mobility. Sedentary people lose mobility because of disuse, just as they lose strength or endurance through disuse. By continuing to stretch regularly, you can maintain mobility much longer. And perform better too.

While stretching is now accepted by competitive athletes as an important way of warming up and avoiding injury, the message hasn't entirely trickled down to weekend athletes, claims Anderson. "You don't see many guys do any kind of real warm-up before playing a softball game," he says. "Tennis is another sport where people walk out onto the court and start whacking the ball. If they get injured, they're often hurt for a long, long time."

This is particularly true for masters athletes, whose ability to heal rapidly fades with aging. Thus, stretching should become a part of every masters athlete's regular training routine. Don, the runner from my high school team, claimed he didn't like to stretch, because, "it hurt."

It hurt only, because he was doing it wrong. Naturally competitive, Don went all-out when he stretched, the same way he ran the 800 meters. I've been guilty of doing the same, particularly when stretching with a group. I want to show how far I can stretch, hardly a good idea since proper flexibility drills involve stretching only to the *edge* of pain, never beyond it. If stretching hurts, you're stretching too hard. For those interested in stretching, whether as a competitor or for general fitness, consider the following advice:

–*Don't bounce.* People attempting to touch their toes sometimes feel they can reach further by going up and down, building up momentum so to speak. That's temporarily true, except the purpose is not to reach further, but rather to get and stay loose. Bouncing *pulls* the muscles, rather than stretches them. Result: the muscles react, and tighten, increasing the risk of injury.

–Don't stretch too far. Too many people look upon stretching as one more activity in which to become competitive. The result can be the injury you're trying to prevent. No-pain-no-gain doesn't work with flexibility. If your muscles hurt during or after your stretching routine, that's because you're stretching too aggressively.

–Follow others cautiously. Even though the ballerina next to you can twist her body to resemble a pretzel, don't feel you need to follow her routine. Most often when I've overstretched, it was because I was stretching in a group with looser-limbed women. Unconsciously, I found myself trying to stretch as far as they did, or copying stretches that proved painful to me. Brown suggests tailoring a program to your own needs. "Most individuals understand the need for stretching," says Brown, "but often they adopt a program they read in a magazine. Not everybody has the same needs for range of motion."

–Warm your muscles first. Starting your workout in warm-up clothes that you shed later is one way to achieve this. Self-massage of specific muscles also can help. But the best time for stretching is in the middle of your warm-up routine. Joggers often are advised to run a mile first, then stop to stretch before continuing the workout. Another time to stretch may be at the end of a hard workout, to loosen tightened muscles so you can exercise again the next day. I stretch most often while soaking post-workout in my basement whirlpool.

–Don't worry about improvement. "You do not have to push limits or attempt to go further each day," says Anderson. Until there is an Olympic medal offered for stretching, most people should not attempt to measure their stretching from day to day.

–*Stretch at odd moments.* Flexibility drills do not need to be limited to the hour a day during which you train. Use other times to relax and do some short stretches. Watch the way a cat or dog stretches. Animals stretch because it feels good, and when they feel like it, not because their fitness coach told them to do so. This is a good approach for humans too. I'll often stretch while sitting at my desk. Riding an up escalator in a department store, I usually drop my heels over the edge of the step to stretch my achilles tendons. You can invent times and places to stretch. Just because you don't see a particular stretch diagrammed in your favorite running magazine doesn't mean it's not good for you.

–*Be gentle.* "Emphasize a gentle range to get a nice little pull," says Brown. Consistent, gentle stretching will do you more good than aggressive flexibility routines done sporadically.

–*Be cautious.* If you have had any recent physical problems or have undergone surgery (particularly of the joints or muscles), check with your physician before starting an exercise routine involving flexibility drills. If you have been inactive for a long time, start slowly.

MASSAGE

While discussing sports booms on a TV talk show in late 1989, the host asked me to predict the sport of the 90s. I considered past and present booms: from tennis to skiing, from jogging to cycling, from aerobic dancing to walking. What's next?

"Massage!" I announced.

That got a good laugh, but I was serious. Not that we're going to swap our running shoes for massage tables, but increasing numbers of fitness athletes have discovered the benefits of sports massage, despite a bad image caused by sexually-oriented "massage parlors." Although massage certainly is *sensual*, but does not need to be sexual.

Whether sport of the 90s or not, massage is hardly new. Fifteen century old cave paintings in the Pyrenees demonstrate a form of massage. Hippocrates recommended in the fourth century B.C. that "the physician must be experienced in rubbing." The modern father of sports massage was Peter Ling, a Swedish fencing instructor, who in 1813 combined massage with exercise into "medical gymnastics."

Swedish massage utilizes oils to reduce friction of the hands on the body in five standard techniques: effleurage (stroking); petrissage (circular motions); tapotement (hacking, cupping); friction (rapid movements to produce heat); and kneading (like kneading bread). Another form of massage is Japanese shiatsu, pressing fingers into points of the body to release trapped energy, or *chi*. Sports massage emphasizes cross-fiber techniques and trigger point work. Massage is as much art as science. My therapist Patty Longnecker admits she borrows from many disciplines.

Those who practice massage in the U.S. prefer to be called massage therapists, rather than *masseur* (male) or *masseuse* (female), or *soigneur*, the appellation for those who service cyclists on the *Tour de France*. The American Massage Therapy Association (A.M.T.A.) contains 7555 certified massage therapists (300 certified in sports massage) and lists 56 approved schools of massage in North America. Only 15 states, however, license therapists.

Relief occurs, because massage hastens the removal from tissues of the metabolic by-products of exercise, squeezing such by-products out of the muscle fibers and back into the bloodstream for recirculation or elimination. Massage also stimulates blood flow, nourishing muscle tissue and increasing joint mobility and flexibility.

Despite statements to the contrary, the purpose of massage is *not* to remove lactic acid, which dissipates within 30 minutes after exercise anyway. "Basically, massage promotes the body's self-healing capabilities," says Gene Arbetter, spokesman for the A.M.T.A.

Although for my post-race massage in San Diego I stripped only to my shorts, massage works best when the patient disrobes totally. Blame it on my Puritan upbringing, but I felt uneasy the first time I used a female massage therapist. (Females now comprise 75 per cent of massage school students.) But reputable therapists deal gently with the hang-ups of patients such as myself. They adeptly maneuver sheets or towels so the person on the table never is uncovered. At a clinic on masters running before the 1988 Twin Cities Marathon, three of the five panelists had regular massage therapists. I used a female therapist; Judy Pickert-Hetkowski used a male therapist, as did Barry Brown. Once you become comfortable with your therapist, that person's sex becomes irrelevant.

Massages do not come cheaply, although once I paid only $10 for an hour's massage at the East Bank Club in Chicago, where prices are kept low as a perk for members. Most practitioners don't expect a tip, although I offered one in the club. The A.M.T.A. identifies $35 per hour as the average price paid for its members' services. That's how much Longnecker charges me. Special techniques like "rolfing" can double the price.

Once lying comfortably beneath sheet or towel, either face-down or on my back, I learned quickly to relax and trust the therapist's instincts as to where to push and probe. Most practitioners use an almond oil, often scented, to lubricate their hands moving over your muscles.

Massage can be painful, particularly if the practitioner probes deeply, or uses cross-fiber techniques. I emerged from one session with an uncertified practitioner at a Minnesota ski resort feeling as though I had been beaten up. This is not an entirely unpleasant experience, but you can–and should–guide your therapist. Warns massage therapist Rich Phaigh of Eugene, Oregon: "If the therapist isn't certified, or licensed, or does not have some competent long-term training, you should never let them perform deep tissue work on your body, because there are a vast number of problems they can cause."

Massage cannot serve as a substitute for training. It can't cure cancer and won't unplug clogged coronary arteries. It can't eliminate arthritis, although it may soften some of the pain. "Not everybody in the medical community is willing yet to accept massage," concedes Steven V. Lorsch, M.D., a physician at Illinois Masonic Medical Center in Chicago. Dr. Lorsch believes in massage, but a cardiologist friend of mine, who serves as medical director for the Old Style Marathon in Chicago, claims he dislikes massage because, "I don't like other people putting hands on my body."

I thought that an interesting position for a doctor, but, admittedly, research that might imply therapeutic benefits to massage is scanty. At the three most recent meetings of the American College of Sports Medicine, only one paper offered any insight on massage. Swedish exercise physiologist Nina Ask tested a group of cyclists at Stockholm's Karolinska Institute and found they performed 11 per cent better after massage than after passive rest.

While at the 1989 World Veterans' Championships, I scheduled a pre-event massage with Rich Phaigh. Since Phaigh previously served as full-time massage therapist for Nike's Athletics West team when it was based in Eugene, he gave massages three days a week to Alberto Salazar, Mary Slaney and other top runners. "With those young athletes," Phaigh explained, "I was mainly concerned that their muscles stayed loose despite their tremendous training loads, so I would work deeply and stretch their muscles out with some pull-relax stretching. We'd usually schedule a massage for several hours after a difficult effort, so they would have enough recovery time before climbing on the table.

"With the more mature athlete, who takes a little longer to recover, and generally doesn't have quite as high a training load, the intensity of the massage changes. I lighten up and try and provide some rejuvenation, flush out the superficial muscle groups and let nature take its course."

Phaigh considers it vital for masters runners to obtain massages, since the older a person gets, the longer it takes for the body to return to homeostasis, a state of internal stability. "If a person can have massages on a regular basis, then the strain on their body from day to day will be diminished greatly," says Phaigh.

Not everybody can afford the luxury of the three massages a week offered the members of Athletics West. In fact, with that club disbanded, even those elite athletes must forego regular massage–or pay the price.

Locating a reputable massage therapist also is not easy. Not everybody has a Rich Phaigh nearby. It took me time to select Longnecker from among several therapists in my area. One quality I sought was sports expertise; her being a runner who also cycled was a plus. I checked with several of her clients, word-of-mouth being the best way to identify a good therapist, according to A.M.T.A. president Robert K. King.[4] He also advises that you check credentials and examine surroundings to assure you haven't wandered by mistake into a massage parlor. Guide the therapist by discussing medical problems before treatment, so he or she knows what body areas to focus on. Continue to provide feedback during the massage.

Length of treatment varies, 40 minutes being sufficient for most people. King warns that you never should endure a treatment which leaves you bruised or exhausted, as had been true with the therapist at the Minnesota ski lodge.

----
4. To locate a therapist near you, contact the A.M.T.A. national information office: 1130 West North Shore Avenue, Chicago, IL 60626; telephone: (312) 761-2682.

"Tell the therapist immediately if too much pressure is being used," says King. Don't wait until you are sore from a hard workout before calling for a massage. "Regular treatments help preserve your well-being," claims King.

Self-massage is an option either between or in place of such regular massages. In performing self-massage, three techniques work well:

1. *Stroking.* A long sliding movement of the hands along the length of the muscle. Begin stroking at the point farthest from the heart and massage towards it. An oil or topical rub will help lubricate your hands, or massage in the shower or a whirlpool. This warms the muscles and increases circulation.

2. *Kneading.* Best on the big muscles like thighs, calves or shoulder tops, you can massage more deeply by squeezing the muscles just like you would knead bread. This pushes muscle fibers together and apart, removing metabolic wastes. As with stroking, squeeze toward the heart.

3. *Friction.* Use circular motions around joints and tendons or around muscles. Apply friction with your fingertips, thumbs, or the fleshy base of the thumbs. This loosens and softens ligaments and tendons around joints. Use moderate pressure. This works well if you have any specific joint aches and pain.

According to Phaigh: "Most practical is to learn how to do the massage yourself, not so you can massage your own body, but so you can instruct someone close to you a few simple techniques to provide a 20-30 minute quick massage over your lower extremities. That's not a difficult massage to give. It's very gentle. It's not stressful. If you can learn how to give that to one another, then you can get a massage from a professional on more sporadic basis just to tune up."

Phaigh notes that Soviet athletes receive massages 300-350 times a year, but recommends quick massages three times a week, or at minimum, after every hard effort or long run. He favors two self-massage techniques. One is compression, simply flattening the muscles between the practitioner's hands and the patient's bones. He would combine that with stroking toward the heart.

You should *not* massage after an acute injury or when the skin is inflamed or broken. People with high blood pressure also should consult with their doctor before using massage or self-massage.

Phaig adds: "Self-massage can do some good, but not as much as having a therapist work on you." After incorporating massage into my training schedule, I agree. In fact, it's addictive. It feels *soooooh* good, regardless of how many miles you ran leading up to your time on the table. Whether or not massage offers that magic button sought by the British athlete in the elevator, I plan to use it–along with stretching–as an important means of maintaining my mobility.

9. MINIMIZING INJURY

The summer of 1989 provided a cornucopian feast for track masters: the Senior Olympics in St. Louis; the Nationals in San Diego; the World Vets in Eugene. After competing in all three, I concluded that what I was witnessing was not eternal youth, but rather the art of survival. Those who continue to excel as masters do not necessarily demonstrate more skill than their rivals. They've simply learned better to avoid the twin problems of injury and indifference that cause so many others to drop early from competition.

I've suffered my share of injuries. Preparing for the 1985 World Vets, I had trained too hard in the spring, straining my left Achilles tendon. I competed in Rome anyway, but the aching tendon nagged me for a year before I finally got smart and stopped running for two months to allow it time to heal.

We are not always smart with our training. Many top masters athletes come and go, one year breaking records and winning medals, the next year so hobbled that they either abandon competition or compete badly. But it's not only masters runners who suffer from injuries. The young fall victim equally. John W. Pagliano, D.P.M., a podiatrist from Long Beach, California, surveyed over 3000 runners and found little difference in rate of injury between those under 40 and those over 40. Nor did older runners necessarily suffer more severe injuries than younger ones.

Dr. Pagliano did find a difference in the *type* of injuries suffered. Younger runners more frequently suffered lower leg and knee injuries. Older runners had a higher incidence of foot and hip-lower back injuries. Asked why the difference, Dr. Pagliano admitted he did not know, unless the reasons were gender-related. (There were very few older women runners in the survey originally presented at the 1984 A.C.S.M meeting.)

Injuries cause a narrowing of the masters ranks. As runners continue to train over the years and decades, they are faced with the inevitably of suffering some sort of injury that may cause them to interrupt training, or drop from the sport. Dr. Pagliano cited plantar fascitis (an irritation of the tendon on the bottom of the foot that connects with the heel) in combination with heel spurs as the most frequent injury among older runners: 17 per cent of the total. I have suffered from plantar fascitis several times in a long career, probably the result of my steeplechasing. The injury often is caused by running up on the balls of your feet, as when hurdling or running uphill. That stretches the fascia, which actually connects the ball and the heel. It causes your heel to ache as though struck by a hammer. A heel pad may help, but the best cure is rest, a diagnosis not all runners accept gracefully.

As we age, we supposedly grow in wisdom. Dr. Pagliano noted that younger runners ran more miles per week relative to older runners. Younger runners also did more speed work. One way to interpret this data is that older runners–having survived–learn to moderate their training to minimize the risk of injury.

Minimizing injury, of course, is one way to improve performance, since only if you avoid, or at least *limit*, injuries can you continue to train and continue to improve. Many talented athletes never fulfill their potential, because they constantly get hurt just as they're getting in shape. (This is true with young runners as well as old.) Others become discouraged because of continuing injuries and resign from the ranks of competitive masters runners. The most successful athletes are those who through superior biomechanics, efficient training methods, luck, or some combination of all three seem never to get injured.

At the University of Florida, Michael L. Pollock, Ph.D. studied a group of walkers who made major improvements in aerobic fitness. As soon as they shifted to jogging, however, they began to experience orthopedic problems. Forty per cent of those over age 50 suffered injuries. "It was age-related," says Pollock, "with 20 per cent of those in the 20-29 category injured and 57 per cent for those over 70."

One woman, described by Pollock as being the fittest aerobically, ran herself into a stress fracture. "She was having a great time running past all the men on the track, but her bones couldn't take the stress," he says.

Kenneth E. Sparks, Ph.D., director of clinical program development for St. Vincent Charity Hospital in Cleveland and member of a world record two-mile relay team in his 20s, resumed hard training as he approached age 40. He returned to 4:16 mile and 2:39 marathon shape, but also needed surgery after injuring an Achilles tendon. "If you've been a competitor in the past, you're used to training on the edge," says Sparks. "This may be all right when young, when you heal rapidly. As you age, you need to train smarter and be more in tune with your body. Every time you go out to run, it could be your last workout, because of an injury."

A rather grim warning, but I recall what happened to Tom Sturak at the 1975 World Vets in Toronto. Tom and I first met at the N.C.A.A. track and field championships in 1952, he running for San Diego State, I for Carleton College. (We both have a lot of miles on our wheels.) In Toronto, I watched Tom start the 800 meter run. On the back stretch, he suddenly reacted as though shot in the leg.

That's almost what happened. Tom's Achilles tendon had snapped; other runners afterwards claimed they could hear the tendon twang like a banjo string. Tom eventually returned to competition, but he seemed to have lost some of his old zip. Possibly it was because he feared pushing himself to the point where a traumatic injury like that might occur again. Can't say as I blame him.

Many, if not most, injuries can be traced to overuse. "Two-thirds of injuries are training errors of some sort," claims Stan James, M.D., an orthopedic surgeon from Eugene, Oregon, best known for the arthroscopic surgery he performed on Joan Benoit several weeks before her victory in the 1984 U.S. Olympic marathon trials. We run too far, too fast, or too soon.

—Running too far. High mileage is a common cause of problems among distance runners, particularly those who run marathons. Masters runners seem less likely than younger runners to fall victim to the lure of 100-mile training weeks, but everyone is susceptible to the urge to do "just a little bit more." After all, running further each day is one way by which we improve, a lesson learned early by every beginning jogger. The down side is that at some point, the runner who piles mile upon mile may self-destruct.

Part of the problem is chronic glycogen depletion, glycogen being the form of glucose stored in the muscles as fuel. Run long and you drain the muscles of glycogen, forcing the body to convert fat for energy. This is fine if your goal is weight loss, but fat is a less efficient fuel. Muscles fatigue and lose their ability to move the extremities through their normal range of motion. Fatigued muscles also are less able to stabilize the joints, or bones.

"As the muscle becomes fatigued," explains Dr. Pagliano, "complimentary muscles and tendons attempt to absorb the additional shock and stabilize the joint area. These structures cannot assume the full duties of the exhausted muscles and they too eventually fatigue."

That is the point when all systems deteriorate and we become injured.

—Running too fast. If high mileage is the *bete noire* for long distance runners, those who run short must beware high speed. Yet every training article (including most I've written) indicate that if you want to improve, you must do speedwork. Repeats, intervals, fartlek: those are the keys to the kingdom of victory. The way to improve performance—as most successful coaches tell us—is first to build an endurance base by running long, then cut your miles and run fast. New Zealand's Arthur Lydiard has successfully preached this pattern for four decades. Fine, but Lydiard suggests a definite shift of training at the end of the distance build-up. Only then does Arthur send his runners to the track to run fast. Those who worship the twin gods of distance and speed, who combine running long with running fast, face the most risk of injury. Speedwork is a way to maintain or improve speed, but it is a double-edged sword.

Part of the problem again is glycogen depletion, which occurs most rapidly during all-out running. Fatigued muscles again fail to protect the joints, but the problem becomes more complicated in that the muscles literally are being assailed from all sides, as well as from within, during fast, anaerobic exercise.

The difference between aerobic and *an*aerobic exercise is that the latter means "without oxygen." The heart cannot pump enough oxygen (fuel) to the muscles (engine), and the result is inefficient combustion. Waste products, including lactic acid (rarely a factor in aerobic exercise), accumulate and the muscles start to seize. Compare the look of the 400 meter runner in the last vs. first 100 meters of his or her race. It is the difference between watching a gazelle and a rhinoceros. In attempting to finish fast, the quarter-miler recruits every available muscle fiber to keep moving forward. Overextended muscles may fail, particularly if they are undertrained.

Among masters athletes the problem is compounded by the fact that as we age, we stiffen. No amount of stretching or massage can entirely prevent the steady deterioration of our tendons and soft tissue. "At the cellular level," explains Dr. Pagliano, "there is collagen degeneration and an increase of friability (fragility) with age. This leads to the 'brittle' tendon syndrome of the veteran athlete." In his study of 3000 long distance runners, Dr. Pagliano found that masters runners developed significantly more soft tissue injuries, especially Achilles tendonitis.

–Running too soon. All of the above can be compounded if you run too far and/or too fast too soon. This can apply to the beginning runner, one who never has participated in the sport, or the born-again runner, one returning to the sport after a long lay-off, or it can apply to the regular runner returning to full-time training after an injury or after resting off-season.

Beginning and born-again runners probably suffer fewer problems, because their goals may be less well defined. If your goal is "fitness" or "getting back in shape," you can pause in your training routine and allow minor injuries to heal. But a seasoned runner, pointing for the Nationals or the World Vets, has an agenda. The seasoned vet is on a timetable. The vet knows from past experience that, since this is June he should be running 20 miles on Sundays, or 10 x 400 meters on the track–and maybe that vet is foolish enough to be doing both while seeking peak performance. Committed runners usually are less patient with injuries and may try to "run through them," ignoring pain. When this occurs, they often convert a minor injury into a major one.

One problem is that different parts of the body develop (or deteriorate) at different rates. Not all training benefits vanish during long layoffs. Fast-twitch muscles hold some of their endurance. Muscle capillaries, which increase by 40-50 per cent in training, remain and retain their ability to eliminate the waste products of exercise, such as lactic acid. Since not all systems of the body detrain or retrain equally, your skeletal system may be tugged in several directions. It may not accept the strain of training at your previous level, particularly as you age.

Cross-training, which involves activities in multiple sports, has been promoted as an effective way to increase training, or rehabilitate from injuries. I'm not certain I believe the effectiveness of the former, although I concede the benefits of the latter. Certainly if unable to run, you can maintain conditioning by pedaling an exercise bike or donning a floating device and jumping in the pool. The problem occurs when you climb *off* the bike or *out* of the pool and resume running. You actually may predispose yourself to reinjury by staying in shape. You can come back too soon.

Carl Foster, Ph.D., director of cardiac rehabilitation and exercise training at Sinai-Samaritan Medical Center warns against overconfidence bred from cross training. "Your cardiac output may be high if you bike or swim or ski, but your muscles and joints may not be ready for the different stresses in running. If you're in good general shape, it's too easy to overdo it, then you're sore and creaky, and you can beat yourself up orthopedically."

Obviously the triple dangers of running too far, too fast or too slow can affect our performance unless we learn to train and race intelligently. Here are some suggestions:

1. *Define.* The best preventative for injury is an appropriate training program, based on logical goals and level of fitness. Dr. James says, "It's important to have a goal and know what you need to do to achieve that goal." Defining your training program well in advance allows you to gradually taper your training, thus avoiding the excesses that so often result in injury. Eighteen months prior to winning the marathon gold medal at the 1981 World Vets, I sat down and planned my training focused on that one race. I concede that often I am not that intelligent or farsighted.

2. *Tailor.* The training program you use must be designed specifically for you, keeping in mind your strengths or weaknesses. A program developed for someone training in San Diego with its constant weather would be different than one for someone training at altitude in Colorado, or where winters are cold in Maine. Availability of tracks or running trails also dictates how and when you train. So does your job or family situation. Although I frequently draft training programs that get printed in a magazine with 445,000 readers, I do so grudgingly knowing that everybody is different. Few of those readers, or the readers of this book, should accept as gospel everything said by me or any other running expert. "It's a mistake to look at somebody successful in your age group and try to mimic their program," warns Dr. James.

3. *Equip.* Dr. Pagliano identifies improper equipment as one major cause of injury. "A lot of runners have a tendency to wear their shoes too long," he says. Worn shoes may fail to offer protection, or may cause an unnatural footstrike. Check soles and heels frequently to guard against wear. The materials used in shoes--particularly the midsoles–deteriorate with age. Shoes that seemed so pliable when examined at the sporting goods store probably have lost much of their cushioning ability 12 months later, even if they don't look worn. Changes in temperature (cold vs. hot weather) also affect a shoes' ability to withstand shock. Finally, know the use for each shoe you wear. Sprinter Irene Obera trains in flats, reserving spikes only for important races. If you're a distance runner going fast in practice, you may be able to stride more safely in a flexible racing flat than in a heavier, training pair.

4. *Avoid.* Learn what causes injury and eliminate that from your training routine. Despite having won two world titles in the 3000 meter steeplechase, I've had to abandon that event. I can't succeed as a steeplechaser without proper training, but I can't train properly (over hurdles and bar-

riers) without dramatically increasing my risk of injury. A high school coach complained about one of his runners who got injured when he ran more than 35 weekly miles. I offered a simple solution: "Have him run 34 miles a week." Our bodies often send us signals that we are unwilling to receive.

5. *Rest.* Former Oregon track coach Bill Bowerman rightfully received credit for initiating the hard-easy approach to training: first day, train hard; second day, rest. But Bowerman didn't limit rest to one day, often prescribing two or three days rest after particularly stressful workouts. Jack T. Daniels, Ph.D., track coach for the State University of New York at Cortland notes that muscle soreness often peaks 48 hours after an extremely hard workout. He suggests two days rest after every hard workout as a preventative to injuries for his college athletes. The Daniels approach makes particular sense for masters athletes.

6. *Monitor.* The best-designed program can be your route to disaster if followed blindly. Just because your pre-planned schedule suggests you should be covering 50 miles a week or speeding quarters in under 75 seconds, you can get yourself into trouble if you fall behind and push to achieve these goals. A cold or minor injury may demand a shift. Have the flexibility to make changes related to the current status of your health. The best monitor is a knowledgeable coach looking over your shoulder; second best is a diary that forces you to analyze your workouts on a regular basis.

7. *Beware.* Don't continue to push hard when injured, even if that injury seems minor. If unduly sore or fatigued, this may be an advance warning of trouble to come. React quickly and take time off, or cut the intensity of your training. Ice and anti-inflammatory drugs are effective remedies for most minor problems, but Dr. James warns: "Don't try to run through pain."

8. *Seek.* Learn the difference between minor injuries and those liable to last long and cost you training time, thus hard-won conditioning. There is a major difference between a muscle that is sore and one that is pulled. Sore muscles occur naturally and gradually during hard work. A pulled muscle is a sudden and traumatic injury. Seek help early from a competent sports professional, whether a trainer or a sports physician. "The medical profession offers excellent specialists," says Roy Benson, a sports consultant from Atlanta, Georgia. "Runners should stop playing around with their injuries and get help quickly." Benson recommends physical therapists as the logical source to begin. "They can't treat or diagnose, but physical therapists can evaluate your injury and refer you to the proper doctor. Once the doctor finds out what's wrong, the therapist can supervise your recovery."

The ultimate secret of success in training, the best way to minimize injuries, is to stop well below the red line of self-destruction. Sometimes you can get most out of your body by training less rather than more. "Nature has a buffer zone where you can maximize training without getting injured," claims Dr. James. "But too many runners fail to identify the limits of that zone. So they're constantly reaching out to discover how far they can take their program. It almost takes an injury to tell them where to stop."

10. MOTIVATION

One night I was changing clothes in the locker room of my local tennis club when a player inquired about the group of people he had seen around me, wanting to know what we were doing.

I explained about the beginning running class I was teaching at the time. The tennis player seemed surprised: "I didn't know you could teach running." He then went on to his activity, and I went on to mine–which at that moment meant going out for pizza with class members.

He was right, of course. You don't need to teach running–or shouldn't need to. Children learn to run almost as soon as they learn to walk. It is only as adults that people forget to run, and sometimes have to be retaught. In most running classes, we are not teaching running; we are teaching motivation.

Motivation is the key to success in any sport, but particularly at the masters level. Most masters athletes do not need motivation to exercise, but they sometimes need motivation to compete, or to succeed in competition.

We compete for a variety of reasons. For some, it offers an opportunity to regain glories lost while young. Others have echoed the theme that competing in sports allows them to remain eternally young. Norton Davey of Playa del Ray, California, an Ironman triathlete in the 65-69 class, claims, "I don't have any more friends my own age any more. All they want to do is sit around and stare at the wall." Norton found he had more in common with young triathletes. Of course, at most masters competitions, everybody acts young. Sociability also can be a motivating factor, the opportunity to renew old sporting acquaintanceships. As one who has competed in seven of the first eight World Veterans Games (missing only Puerto Rico in 1983 because of injury), I'm motivated by a desire to see old friends, even if only every other year.

What motivates other masters to compete? Consider some of the possibilities:

HEALTH. This is probably the primeval reason providing motivation for so many beginners in their jogging or fitness routines. Like Ponce de Leon, they are seeking the Fountain of Youth. They expect to live longer. And there is strong evidence to suggest that this, indeed, may be the case.

At various times, running has been touted as good for everything that ails us. Thomas J. Bassler, M.D., a Los Angeles pathologist, once even proposed that by finishing a marathon you would be immune from heart attacks for six months. His reasoning was that in order to finish 26 miles 385 yards, you would modify your lifestyle enough to eliminate most of the risk factors involved in heart attacks. You'd stop smoking, improve your diet, etc. There was a certain inherent logic in Dr. Bassler's arguments that appealed to a lot of people wanting to justify those 20-mile workouts on Sunday.

Inevitably, Dr. Bassler's immunity theory, if not totally disproved, at least was discarded as too absolute. Meanwhile Ralph Paffenbarger, M.D. offered convincing epidemiological evidence that Harvard alumni who exercised lived several years longer than those who did not. Some experts consider Dr. Paffenbarger's conclusions unfounded. Nevertheless, the quest for the Fountain of Youth has motivated many to begin exercise programs; some eventually become highly motivated competitive masters athletes.

VIGOR. Whether or not you'll live longer, says George Sheehan, M.D., you'll live and feel better. Dr. Sheehan, Medical Editor for *Runner's World*, has been diagnosed as having prostate cancer. He concedes that eventually it will kill him, maybe two years down the road, maybe 20. Meanwhile, he's living life at its fullest, enjoying his regular runs, competing in triathlons, and continuing to promote running as a way of life, quoting Sartre and Socrates rather than Bassler and Paffenbarger.

George ran several middle distance races at the 1989 World Vets. He placed in none, but left Eugene enthused over how close he had come to a medal. When I had visited George a few months earlier at his home in Ocean Grove, New Jersey, he hardly acted the role of one terminally ill. We went for a run on the boardwalk on a marvelously sunny day, the sound of surf in our ears, seagulls fluttering over-head. The ability to remain vigorously active, and the desire to remain so for the rest of our lives, keeps many of us run-ning. A comedian once joked that joggers were simply going to "die in good health." That's a funny gag line, but consider the alternative: Would you rather spend your final years in poor health?

One of my warmest memories as a masters athlete was that of Duncan MacLean, who ran the sprints at the first few World Veterans' Championships. In 1977 in Gothenburg, Sweden, MacLean ran 21.7 for 100 meters, not bad for someone in his 90s. Later during the week, my wife and I were strolling through Tivoli Gardens, when Duncan passed in the company of a younger athlete, someone in his 60s. Judging from his youthful stride, Duncan seemed hardly older than that age himself. The picture of Duncan MacLean, still vigorous at age 90, remains with me, serving as very strong motivation to stay active.

FUN. While "fitness" is the catch-all excuse that causes many to start exercise routines, that is too abstract a concept to keep them in the sport long. Certainly, fitness is insufficient motivation to send a man in his 50s to the run-way of the triple jump. Masters who demonstrate competi-tive longevity do so because it adds to their overall enjoy-ment. They find running fun. Call it a throwback to the games we played as kids if you want, but we like to run because we like to run. To paraphrase Yogi Berra: The Games aren't over until the games are over. Nobody said adults couldn't have fun.

RELEASE. The ability of exercise to relieve stress has been well documented by sports scientists. William P. Morgan, Ed.D. of the University of Wisconsin at Madison suggests as one reason for this release the "time-out effect." You escape all your pressures by working out. You construct a cocoon that insulates you from stress. The telephone can't disturb you; your boss can't lay another pile of work on your desk.

But it's more than that. In collaboration with Morgan, James M. Rippe, M.D., a cardiologist at the University of Massachusetts medical school, tested walkers on a treadmill at various paces, giving them psychological tests before and after. Dr. Rippe noted that anxiety and tension decreased immediately after the walk. This improved mood continued for several hours later. So-called "runner's high"—not necessarily experienced by every runner on every run—has been connected with the body's release of pain-relieving chemicals to anesthetize the brain. With the exception of overly competitive athletes for whom the drive for success may create its own stress, most people find that exercise leaves them relaxed afterwards.

During a recent workout with the high school cross country team I coach, everybody started sluggish, the result of a day spent in classes plus tired muscles from a hard run the day before. We ran a half hour at an easy pace. Toward the end one of the girls, Christina Galaviz, commented, "Now that we're stopping, I finally feel like I want to run."

Of course, that's one of the reasons we run; that feeling of release keeps us coming back each day.

GLORY. Don't overlook the thrill of victory as a strong motivational factor. The agony of defeat is nowhere near as agonizing as in the fabled film clip on A.B.C.'s

"Wide World of Sports" of a ski jumper tumbling off the jump. As later stories revealed, the jumper, a Yugoslav, was not even injured during his cataclysmic spill. He went on to jump again, and on the 25th anniversary of the program admitted to reporters he couldn't understand why he was so famous in the United States.

The call to glory, the opportunity to stand on the top step with a medal around our necks, motivates many of us. One afternoon I invited Jeffrey L. Samelson, Ph.D., a psychologist in Michigan City, Indiana, to talk to my cross country team. He presented a relaxation drill that involved each runner selecting a word, a "mantra," that they could repeat over and over to themselves while getting ready to compete. He asked what word they might use.

One of the runners on my boys' team that had suffered through a losing season offered the word: "Finish."

But Elizabeth Galaviz, Christina's younger sister and the top runner on a very successful girls' team, quickly suggested: "Win!"

That was one of the reasons for Elizabeth's success. She had learned to motivate herself to run very well. Whether or not all of us select "win" as our mantra, glory remains a strong motivational factor for many who compete as masters.

FULFILLMENT. David L. Costill, Ph.D., director of the human performance laboratory at Ball State University and a top-ranked masters swimmer, believes most masters compete for reasons more psychological than physiological. "I've always been very goal oriented," Costill explains. "It motivates me to succeed, whether in my work or in the pool. But competition for masters more often is you against yourself rather than against anybody else."

Inevitably, it comes down to that. Everybody competes against his or her own potential. Whether or not I win an award in my age category at the World Vets depends in part whether or not Norm Green, Ray Hatton or someone else of their caliber appears on the starting line. At most races in my area, my arrival at the check-in table similarly signals to a number of other fine masters that, today, they probably must settle for the lesser trophy. Many of our victories, thus, are subject to chance.

Less subject to chance is the fulfillment obtained from having tried to the best of your ability, having made the most of what you came with. That should motivate all of us to stay in competition–if only within ourselves–for the rest of our lives.

11. A MASTERS DIET

David E. Martin, Ph.D., a sports scientist at Georgia State University and consultant for the U.S. Olympic Committee, is not a dietitian, but often finds athletes approaching him for nutritional advice. "I tell them it's not just carbohydrate loading before a marathon," says Martin. "Good nutrition is a year-round situation, and it's the same whether you want to be a healthy person or a healthy athlete."

Does better nutrition result in better performances? What is good nutrition for someone seeking sports glory? Does sports nutrition differ measurably from "nutrition nutrition," the diet supposedly good for us all? Also, what about vitamins, minerals and so-called "performance enhancing pills" often pitched to athletes? These are questions that most masters would like answered.

While researching an article on sports nutrition for *Hippocrates* prior to the 1988 Olympic Games, I interviewed Robert O. Voy, M.D., then director of the U.S. Olympic Committee's division of sports medicine and science. "The goal," Dr. Voy explained, "is not to create some super-diet that guarantees gold medals, but rather to assure that our athletes will not fail for reasons that can be controlled."

So what we need is a fail-safe diet. Talk to any dietitian, and they will identify the proper balance of foods as: 55-65 per cent carbohydrate, 10-15 per cent protein, and 25-35 per cent fat. "The percentages differ slightly, depending on who you talk to," says Nancy Clark, R.D., a dietitian with Sports Medicine, Brookline in Massachusetts, "but those numbers form the gold standard for sports as well as for standard nutrition." Clark, author of "Nancy Clark's

Sports Nutrition Guidebook," says, "It makes little difference whether you run in the World Vets, or watch from the stadium seats."

Still, while the *general* principles of sound nutrition differ little between Weight Watchers and Olympians, certain *specifics* do differ. "Athletes are told to avoid junk foods," admits Ann C. Grandjean, Ed.D., director of the International Center for Sports Nutrition, "but the reality is that if you are eating 4000 calories a day for an endurance sport, once you have taken in those first 2000 calories–assuming you've done a reasonably intelligent job of selecting foods–you've probably obtained all the nutrients you need. You don't need to worry about vitamins and minerals, because you've already supplied your needs. You can afford foods high in sugar, so-called 'empty calories,' because you need energy. Your problem sometimes is finding enough time to eat."

Meanwhile, Jacqueline Berning, R.D., a nutritional advisor for the U.S. Swim Team, tells athletes that fast cars run on Super Unleaded, not diesel fuel. "You can't put diesel fuel into a Porsche and expect it to run fast," says Berning. "It doesn't make sense to train hard, then make lousy fuel choices. I don't care how fit you are; you're not going anywhere."

Clark, Grandjean, Berning and other sports nutritionists suggest that athletes should eat the "wide variety of lightly processed foods" proclaimed by dietitians as necessary for good health. Athletes also need to balance their diets with foods from all four of the basic food groups. Eat in such a manner, say the experts, and you can maximize performance.

Diet is particularly important for endurance athletes. Fred Brouns of the Nutrition Research Center at the University of Limburg in the Netherlands studied cyclists competing in the *Tour de France*, both in the laboratory and during the race. Brouns discovered that those finishing up front were those most successful at managing their diets. "Endurance athletes must pay close attention to food intake if they expect to keep energy levels high," says Brouns.

One advantage held by such athletes is weight control. If you begin to exercise and do not increase the amount of food consumed, you will lose weight. If you burn approximately 1750 calories a week through exercise, you will lose half a pound a week, two pounds a month, 24 pounds in a year.[5] Most dietitians now concede that cutting food intake by dieting is not enough; the only way to remove weight–and keep it off–is to combine diet *and* exercise. Indeed, some researchers such as Peter D. Wood, Ph.D. of the Stanford Center for Research in Disease Prevention, speculate that the major reason why the exercising members in Dr. Paffenbarger's study of the Harvard alumni lived longer is that they may have succeeded better in controlling their weight, an important risk factor for coronary heart disease.

As long ago as 1867, the U.S. Government backed efforts to promote better nutrition. In 1941, a National Nutritional Conference developed the first set of Recommended Dietary Allowances (R.D.A.'s) for nutrients. In 1977, the Senate Select Committee on Nutrition and Human Needs studied the health problems of American and came up with a series of recommendations for changing our diets for better health. A series of "Dietary Guidelines for Americans" was published in 1985 by the U.S. Department of Health and Human Services. Most recently, these guidelines were included in "The Surgeon General's Report on Nutrition and Health," published in 1988.

There are seven dietary guidelines:

1. *Eat a Variety of Foods.* For good health, you need more than 40 different nutrients, including vitamins and minerals, amino acids (from proteins), essential fatty acids

----

5. Cyclists in Brouns' Tour de France study needed to consume near 8000 calories a *day* merely to balance calories burned.

(from fats and oils). You also need sources of energy. Carbohydrates provide the most efficient source of energy for athletes, because "carbs" convert quickly into the glucose burned by the body as energy. The body will also convert fats and proteins, although somewhat less efficiently.

Most foods contain several nutrients, but except for human milk during the first few months of life, no single food supplies all essential nutrients. For example, milk provides little iron; meat contains almost no calcium. To obtain an adequate diet, you must eat different foods.

Joanne Milkereit, a dietitian associated with the Medical University of South Carolina, advises that every athlete–professional or recreational–tape the following advice to the door of his or her refrigerator: *Eat a wide variety of lightly processed foods.* That may be the best nutritional advice for masters as well. Do this by selecting foods each day from each of the major food groups: 1) fruits; 2) vegetables; 3) Whole-grain and enriched breads, cereals and other products made from grains;[6] 4) milk, cheese, yogurt, and other products made from milk; and 5) meats, fish, poultry, eggs, and dry beans and peas.

The Surgeon General also advises against consuming excessive amounts of any nutrient, or supplement. "You will rarely need to take vitamin or mineral supplements if you eat a variety of foods," state the Dietary Guidelines for Americans. More on that later.

2. *Maintain Desirable Weight.* According to the Surgeon General, obesity affects 34 million adults aged 20 to 74. Most affected are the poor and minorities. If you are overweight, you increase your chances of developing various chronic disorders, including high blood pressure, strokes and diabetes. Some suggest obesity as a disease of inactivity, al-

----

6. The most popular grain eaten by runners is spaghetti, usually eaten before their marathons. Most forms of pasta are made from wheat. Another popular grain is rice.

though proof remains lacking because of the difficulty of evaluating home activity. Too little weight also is a problem, but more people need to lose pounds than gain.

For most masters athletes, obesity is not a major problem. We are perceived by the general population as being a skinny lot. Even among the so-called "whales" who hurl the shot and discus in World Vets competition, their bulk is more often muscle than fat. Still, reductions of even a few pounds of *excess* weight can improve performance. If a distance runner has five pounds of unnecessary fat, it is like donning a five-pound pack each time he races.

To reduce weight, you must eat fewer calories than you burn. Either choose foods with fewer calories, increase physical activity—or both.

To control overeating, eat slowly, take smaller portions, and avoid taking second helpings. To lose weight, eat foods that are low in calories and high in nutrients, such as fruits, vegetables and grains.

You can become too thin. The body needs some fat to survive, and a person who has 5 per cent body fat is not necessarily fitter than someone at 10 per cent. Everyone has an "ideal" body weight; losing too many pounds may cause declines in performance. The only way to determine your best weight is not by various charts, but by weighing yourself regularly and noting how much you usually weigh at the time you achieve your best performances.

My normal weight is 142. On a few occasions when I have gotten out of shape, my weight has climbed as high as 150. Some of my best performances have come when I weighed between 136 and 138, but in 1964, when my weight dropped to 131 because of excessive training, I became injured and lost a chance to qualify for the Olympic team, despite having run the second fastest marathon by an American that same year.

Weight sometimes fluctuates depending on the season. During the winter, the body often adds a protective layer of fat as insulation against the cold. Despite your level of fitness, you weigh more. Summer brings hot weather, causing some of that protective fat layer to melt. But excessive sweating causes temporary dehydration so that if you get on the scales immediately after a hot workout, you may seem to weigh less than you actually do. Minor, seasonal fluctuations in weight are natural and should not cause either despair or hope.

3. *Avoid too much fat, saturated fat and cholesterol.* High blood cholesterol has been identified as one of the major risk factors for coronary heart disease. Eating too much fat is one reason why people have blood cholesterol levels over 200. Fats are found in meat, but also in palm and coconut oils. To limit dietary cholesterol, choose chicken, turkey and fish as well as *lean* cuts of beef, pork and lamb (which contain more iron than poultry). Broiling, steaming and baking are preferable to frying. Use dried beans and grains often as protein sources. Avoid adding too much fat while preparing foods. Try herbs or lemon juice to flavor vegetables. Cholesterol is found only in animal foods. There is no cholesterol in any plant foods. Organ meats, fatty meats and eggs are particularly rich in cholesterol. These foods need not necessarily be purged from your diet, but they should be consumed in moderation.

Some athletes, knowing the link between exercise and an improved cholesterol profile, assume they can avoid the blood tests used to determine risk. Not true. One member of my running club, Mary Taylor, assumed that until a blood test revealed her cholesterol level at 350. Mary's problem was diet. Coming from a Lebanese background, she consumed a diet high in fat. She would eat the fat that others at the table trimmed from their steaks. Mary noted that many of her relatives died young.

Motivated by the test, Mary quickly changed diet. We coach the high school cross country team together. On the way home from a meet one evening, we stopped at a fast food joint. While most team members ordered shakes and burgers, Mary and I headed for the salad bar. With her new and enlightened diet, she had reduced her cholesterol to 200!

(Postscript: Mary and I did some diet education with our team. As a result, they voted to abandon fast food stops and now pack snack lunches to away meets. Kids sometimes have more sense than adults give them credit for. They just need a reason to do things.)

4. *Eat foods with adequate starch and fiber.* Foods high in starch are good sources of energy for athletes. As example, most runners preparing for a marathon eat spaghetti the night before their race. Lately, football players have begun to do the same. The American diet is relatively low in fiber. Eating foods that contain complex carbohydrates provide you with more more fiber as well as more energy. Fiber reduces constipation (although the other side of that coin is flatulence). Still under study is the suggestion that dietary fiber can reduce the risk of certain types of cancer, specifically colon cancer. Steven N. Blair, P.E.D. of the Institute for Aerobics Research in Dallas has offered some convincing epidemiological evidence that such is the case, but the jury of his peers is still out.

5. *Avoid too much sugar.* Table sugar, honey and molasses should be used in moderation. Beware soft drinks. Choose fruit juice instead. If you are very thirsty after a workout, drink water. However, endurance athletes who burn (thus must consume) calories by the thousands often must turn to sugar drinks as the most efficient means of replenishing glycogen stores. Several high-energy drinks serve such a purpose. I've always considered it anachronistic

when I see runners after a long race on a hot day consuming diet soft drinks. That is probably the *one* time when they might benefit from a drink high in sugar content.

But only if they maintain their nutritional house at other times of the day with the well-balanced meals necessary for good health and good performance. Sugars provide calories, but few nutrients. The most significant health problem from eating too much sugar is tooth decay. It's not how much sugar you eat, but how *often* you eat. Most harmful are sweets between meals. Many foods we eat contain some sugar, so brushing your teeth after meals can help control tooth decay.

6. *Avoid too much sodium.* Table salt contains sodium and chlorine, both essential to the diet, but the average American eats six times as much salt as he needs. Many processed foods (those that come in the cardboard boxes) also contain salt for preservation. One hazard for those with too much sodium from salt in their diet is high blood pressure.

Although masters athletes might worry that they lose salt when they sweat, they can replace any such loss adequately simply by following a balanced diet. Reduce the amount of salt you use while cooking or baking. Eat less, or fewer, salty foods such as ham, sausage and potato chips. And don't reach so often for the salt shaker.

7. *If you drink alcoholic beverages, do so in moderation.* Alcoholic beverages are high in calories and low in nutrients. Not only do heavy drinkers develop diseases such as cirrhosis of the liver, but they also develop nutritional deficiencies. The same mind-numbing properties of alcohol that make driving while drunk dangerous also can diminish your athletic ability

Often I enjoy a cold beer after a hot race, but usually I down the beer only after having consumed equal or double the volume in other liquids first. One problem about alcoholic drinks such as beer is that they serve as diuretics, thus can increase the post-race problems of dehydration.

Why should we follow the advice of the guidelines contained in the Surgeon General's report? Masters athletes sometimes believe that we are immune to heart attacks and related health problems because of our lifestyles, which often includes an hour or more of vigorous exercise a day. While this may be partially true, we will obtain maximum benefit only if our lifestyles also include good dietary habits.

FOOD FADDISM

What about supplements? Can masters athletes improve performance by use of various pills, whether vitamins or minerals or any of the other products often promoted in body building magazines, and lately in masters publications? The Dietary Guidelines for Americans recommend against supplementation, boosting instead the variety of foods normally essential for good health. Ironically, surveys of the nutritional habits of elite athletes indicate that those needing supplements the least often use them the most. Various studies of American, Canadian and Irish athletes show that anywhere from 45 to 84 percent use supplementation. Why? Sports nutritionist Grandjean speculates: "If you are interested in what you eat, you are going to be at least aware of supplements. On the other hand, if you never think about nutrition, you probably are not. When you sit down with athletes with bad diets, they usually don't have many questions. Whereas the ones watching what they eat, often bring in their shoe box full of supplements and want to go through all of them."

A less charitable interpretation of the food faddism rampant among athletes is that they will use any means—legal or illegal—to get ahead of their competition.

Witness the use of steroids and blood-doping by young athletes seeking Olympic victory at any cost. Those close to the masters movement believe that athletes over 40 also are guilty of using illegal aids, although nobody yet wants to assume the immense cost of policing the problem. Grandjean suggests that often it is not the best athletes who seek to succeed through supplementation, but rather lower level athletes looking for any means to success.

So even though athletes eat well-balanced meals, they worry that it is not enough. Fads come and go and at various times wheat germ, bee pollen or various vitamins and minerals rise and wane in popularity. Most recently, subscribers to *National Masters News* have been deluged with ads for energy capsules touted as the route to sports success–but at a high price, nearly $200 for a three-month supply. Most research suggests the capsules are worthless for improving performance.

It is because athletes believe–or at least *hope*–supplements can enhance their performance, that they tend to use more supplements than the public at large. Surveys to the contrary, Grandjean detects a lessening of what she calls "overnutrition," at least among the top class of athletes. "Athletes often are ten years ahead of the general public in terms of their eating habits," she says. "Maybe this presages an improvement in nutritional habits for all of us."

SENIOR SNACKING

Do masters athletes have dietary needs different from other athletes, or different from the general public? The image many Americans have of the nutritional habits of senior citizens is little old ladies snacking on TV dinners because of the boredom of dining alone. Not true, says Elizabeth Brewster, a retired dietitian from the University of Minnesota. Brewster claims that people over 60 have better eating habits than their children and grandchildren.

In a study published in the May 1987 *Journal of the American Dietetic Association*, a research group led by Brewster analyzed the diets of 5640 individuals. The study had been designed to determine what different food groups most people ate, but when researchers compared eating habits across age groups, they discovered that older people were more likely to choose nutritious foods than those younger.

People over 60 most often chose whole grain products: 37 per cent vs. 24 per cent for those aged 20-59. They ate somewhat more "quick breads," including waffles, pancakes and tortillas. More over-60 people (34 per cent) consumed poultry than did members of any other age group. They were less likely to eat sweets and considerably less likely to drink sweetened beverages: only 16 per cent vs. 60 per cent for those under 20. If they drank alcohol, they more often favored wine over beer, although more men over 60 drank hard liquor. Brewster didn't claim older people were wiser than those younger, but suggested, "Maybe they learned something about good nutrition along the way."

A less charitable interpretation of the Minnesota data could be that individuals with poor dietary habits are less likely to live to age 60. This could tip the nutritional scales in favor of smart senior snackers.

Dietitian Nancy Clark agrees that masters athletes should follow the same sound nutritional diet recommended by the Surgeon General, but underlines that advice by adding, "As people get older, they sometimes fail to absorb vitamins and minerals from food as well. It's even more important for masters athletes to choose high quality foods than young athletes."

Clark's list of favorite foods for masters includes vegetables such as broccoli, spinach, green peppers, tomatoes and potatoes. She recommends low-fat dairy products: skim milk, low-fat cheeses such as mozzarella, and low-fat yogurt. She suggests lean mean for iron and the zinc.

Fiber-rich foods, such as whole wheat breads and grain cereals also make good meals for masters athletes, says Clark, who adds:

"Sometimes younger athletes can get away with junk-food diets, but older ones should be particularly careful, knowing nutrients are absorbed less well the older they get. This also fits into a good-health approach. As we get older, we become more concerned about heart health and high blood pressure. A good sports diet is also a heart-healthy diet."

Clark claims that there is no increased need for masters athletes to take vitamin and mineral supplements. "You can get all the nutrients you need from well-balanced meals," she states in conclusion.

12. INCREASING YOUR YOUTHSPAN

The number of years we live has increased steadily, from an average lifespan of 26 years in the Stone Age to 70.3 today for the average American man, 78 for the average woman. Americans might logically use the old gag line: "If I knew I was going to live this long, I'd have taken better care of myself."

But *how* should we take care of ourselves? What should we do to increase not merely our lifespan, but our youthspan? Many masters athletes are less worried about living longer lives than we are in continuing to perform–both on and off the track. There is a link between human performance in both arenas. Inevitably researchers point to "exercise habits," including athletic competition, as a major factor affecting how we survive into old age. Indeed, many of the problems of aging are not caused by disease, but by deconditioning. By exercising, by staying in shape, by competing in masters track, we extend the years of our youth.

How can you extend your youthspan, if not lifespan? Following are a ten areas where aggressively exercising masters athletes keep themselves young:

1. MUSCLE: As we age, we lose muscle. With the decline in muscle comes a decline in strength, most noticeable among people past 60. After age 30, muscle fibers decrease at a rate of 3 to 5 per cent each decade. This can result in a loss of up to 30 per cent of muscle power by age 60, according to David L. Costill, Ph.D. of Ball State University. "It's a case of use it or lose it," says Costill. By exercising the body, you retain strength longer.

2. BONE: Mona M. Shangold, M.D. believes Whistler's mother had osteoporosis, pointing to the bent-over position of the lady in the painting by James Whistler. "She spent all that time sitting in the chair," says Dr. Shangold. "If she had gotten up to jog, it might have prevented her problem."

Those who exercise suffer less from osteoporosis, a degenerative disease that weakens bones and results not only in dowagers' humps, but also in 700,000 fractures a year, mostly hip. It is a disease that affects older women, but men are not immune–assuming they live into their 80s. And whether or not you suffer from osteoporosis, everyone suffers from bone loss as they age. Limiting bone loss will keep you young. Drinking milk and estrogen supplementation (for women) can help, but physical exercise is equally important. "There's no doubt that exercise is beneficial to the bones," says Barbara L. Drinkwater, Ph.D. of Pacific Medical Center. "Active people maintain bone better; we lose it less rapidly." This is true for individuals in their 20s, but even those who have not begun to exercise until later in life can significantly improve density.

3. FAT: According to Jack H. Wilmore, Ph.D. of the University of Texas at Austin, beginning at age 25, the average American adds 1.5 pounds of body fat per year. This gain of fat may not be entirely reflected in the person's gain in total weight, since some of the fat gain is balanced by loss of lean body mass (muscle and bone, as above).

Those who exercise resist this fattening trend. Wilmore suggests that the average jogger or walker (one who covers 10-15 miles a week) probably only adds a quarter pound of fat a year. More active exercisers in those or other fitness activities do a better job of avoiding increased body fat, thus resist this symptom of old age.

4. CAPACITY: Another symptom of aging is a decline of work capacity, measured in the laboratory through downward changes in the volume of oxygen con-

sumed per minute during all-out effort. Since muscles consume most of the oxygen during exercise, any reduction in muscle mass reduces maximal oxygen consumption. Other factors affecting capacity, according to Everett L. Smith, director of the Biogerontology Laboratory in the University of Wisconsin's department of preventative medicine, include the capability of the heart and lungs. But though aging causes a definite loss of work capacity, sedentary individuals can regain much of what they lost. Smith states, "It is possible to regain up to 50 percent of the loss of cardiovascular function with regular exercise."

By exercising regularly, you blunt the decline. Michael L. Pollock, Ph.D., of the University of Florida has studied a group of masters runners over an 18-year period. He notes that their decline in work capacity is only half that of sedentary people: 5 per cent a decade, or a half a percent a year. Among those who continue to train at the same intensity, there is virtually no decline.

5. FLEXIBILITY: As we age, we stiffen. Moving becomes more difficult. This loss of flexibility ages our appearance. Smith identifies connective tissue changes in muscle, ligaments, joint capsules, and tendons as being responsible for 98 percent of flexibility loss. He adds: "The decline of flexibility, however, is more strongly correlated to disuse than to age degeneration."

Katie M. Munn studied 20 individuals with an average age of 72 over a period of a dozen weeks at the University of Wisconsin. They did light stretching exercises, mostly while seated in chairs. With even that little exercise, the participants increased range of motion in their necks by 28 percent, in the wrists by 13 percent, in their shoulders by 8 percent, in their hips and back by 12 percent and in their ankles by 48 percent. By warming up properly and stretching afterwards, people involved in aerobic activity demonstrate much greater flexibility than those who fail to exercise.

6. HEART: You can only look and feel young if you stay alive. Beginning in the late 50s, a group led by Martha L. Slattery, Ph.D. of the University of Utah Medical School in Salt Lake City studied the health history and leisure-time physical activity of 3043 railroad workers, some in strenuous jobs, some in sedentary occupations. Slattery discovered what numerous other studies into the habits of everyone from London transport workmen to Harvard alumni to San Francisco longshoremen has shown: those who exercise lived longer.

"You do not require a lot of activity to get a protective effect," says Slattery. Her statistics showed that men who expended 1000 or more kilocalories a week in leisure-time physical activity showed lower death rates from diseases of the heart and blood vessels. That work load is the equivalent of three to four hours a week in some moderately intense exercise such as weeding the garden–or running 10 miles. "The greatest increase in protection was between those men who were sedentary and those who had some activity," Slattery says.

7. LUNGS: The respiratory *muscles*, rather than the lungs, are the major benefactors of exercise. They adapt to exercise as do the leg muscles. The shortness of breath experienced by people out of shape is not so much that their lungs are not working correctly, as it is the fatiguing of muscles responsible for moving air in and out of those lungs. "As you age, the chest wall stiffens and you also lose the elastic tissue in your lungs," states Donald A. Mahler, M.D. of Dartmouth Medical School. "You can't exhale air as quickly compared to a younger person."

For inactive people, who have lost flexibility in their rib cages, it's another example of aging through disuse, rather than disease. Dr. Mahler often sees patients over 60 who complain of shortness of breath, but with no pathological cause. Easy aerobic exercise, such as walking, often is enough to improve their problem.

8. SOCIABILITY: Although many people exercise at home, fitness can be a very social activity. Lester Breslow, M.D., a professor with the School of Public Health at the University of California at Los Angeles, directed a study of nearly 7000 men and women in Alameda County, California that lasted 25 years. Dr. Breslow identified seven different health practices–among them drinking and smoking–that negatively affected mortality. But he also identified sociability as a factor affecting youth. Among the men with the fewest social contacts, the death rate doubled. Among women, it tripled. A similar increase in mortality was noted among those who expressed the least satisfaction with life.

"What we found," says Dr. Breslow, "was that the strength of a person's social network–friends as well as relatives–had just about as much relationship to subsequent mortality as did the adherence to these health-related habits." In the sense that exercise promotes sociability, it can keep us young.

9. BRAIN: One factor affecting youthfulness is mental attitude: if we consider ourselves old, we act old. Having physical fitness as a goal certainly helps maintain a positive attitude toward aging, but some evidence suggests that running may make us smarter, may help prevent brain fade. Marian Diamond, Ph.D. of the University of California, Berkeley demonstrated the effects of stimulation on the brain by comparing rats placed in an isolated, sedentary environment with active rats who exercised on a treadmill. Rats, even older rats, from the active setting, solved the problem of maze running (a form of intelligence testing) much better than those from the sedentary group.

"The nerve cell can adapt like a muscle cell," says Diamond. "With use, it grows and becomes more efficient." Rats are similar to other mammals–including humans–in their brain structure. Thus, humans may be able to stimulate brain cells by exercising too. Currently, Diamond's lab is studying how much this apparent increase in intelligence is due to exercise and how much to the stimulation that comes with exercise.

10. STRESS: In a final category related to maintaining youth, exercise can help reduce the stresses of aging. Herbert A. deVries, Ph.D., the retired director of the Andrus Gerontology Center at the University of Southern California, tested how ten elderly people responded to mild electric shock. Following exercise, their shock response decreased 18 percent.

High blood pressure has always been one index of stress. Researchers at the Institute for Aerobics Research in Dallas, placed a group of young men with high blood pressure on a 16-week exercise program involving walking, jogging or running. Their blood pressures dropped. Those with the highest pressures dropped the most.

Exercise certainly is no panacea for all man's ills, although Pollock states: "If you can avoid injuries and stay motivated, the changes attributed to aging can be held off for a long time. It then becomes a matter of pure aging versus the aging that takes place just because we're doing less."

13. A GATHERING OF GREYHOUNDS

Nelson Gomes da Silva of Brazil broke sharply from the staggered lanes, gliding into a two-stride lead over Australian Alan Bradford. Six other World Vets finalists struggled to keep up. The smooth Brazilian's time at 200 meters: 29 seconds.

As the lead runners turned into the home straightaway, Hayward Field began to rock with staccato applause from nearly 5000 people jamming the west stands. *Clap! Clap! Clap! Clap! Clap!* Da Silva reached 400 meters ahead of Bradford in 59 seconds: a pace, which if continued would break the world record!

For the pair were not young milers for whom such speed might seem, well, pedestrian, but rather *masters*, racing in the Eighth World Veterans' Championships in Eugene, Oregon. They were competitors in "M50," the five-year division for men aged 50 to 54. They were running not the mile (or its metric equivalent, the 1500), but rather 800 meters. And as track announcer Al Sheahen quickly informed the crowd, "The two-minute barrier has never been broken by an over-50 half-miler!"

The Eugene fans reacted by raising the pitch of their support. CLAP! CLAP! CLAP! CLAP! CLAP! Oregon's venerable, wooden stadium used for three U.S. Olympic Trials and numerous national championships echoed with cheers as the balding Bradford closed on da Silva. Passing the spent Brazilian going into the final turn, Bradford kicked home under a crescendo of noise, a few ticks over two minutes (2:00.40), failing to break that barrier though not the world record.

The crowd sighed its disappointment–*but wait!* Another group of half-milers moved onto the track, the finalists in M45. Don Parker of Pasadena, California won in 1:59.04; Great Britain's Peter Browne followed with a 1:55.20 victory in M40. Then on to complete a series of 5000 meter races; fastest was Kenyan Wilson Waigwa, M40: 14:26.43.

Surely, it must be every meet promoter's dream to stage a series of races that get progressively faster. Such is the way of masters track, beginning with the older groups (women before men) and moving to the younger. This scenario produced in Eugene a succession of marvelously exciting races. Attending a masters track meet, in fact, might be compared to attending the greyhound races. The competitors (masters and greyhounds) arrive at the starting line in large packs, unpublicized, identifiable only by numbers on their flanks. But once the gun sounds, it matters not. The racing is furious.

Bradford's win was but one highpoint on an evening featuring–*bing, bing, bing*–19 finals in the 800. It came during an 11-day orgy (July 27 to August 6, 1989) of 450 track, field and road events, heats and finals, utilizing two tracks (the second being a high school oval in neighboring Springfield), involving a record 4951 athletes from 58 countries, who won 2000 gold, silver and bronze medals in a salute to senior sports witnessed, for the first time, by surprisingly large numbers of spectators, an estimated 50,000 over the length of the meet.

At most masters meets, those in the stands are usually relatives or fellow competitors, a handful at most. At the two previous World Veterans' Championships, utilizing mammoth stadiums in Rome and Melbourne, the lack of local interest in aging athletes was painfully evident from rows of empty seats. Eugene's Hayward Field with its 14,000 capacity provided a more intimate setting. Hayward was near full for the opening ceremonies and half full on several other days. Many spectators were competitors between events, but many were not. At the opening ceremonies, Eugene Mayor Jeff Miller asked, "How many come from the community?" Four out of five stood.

Greyhound factor or not, masters track may not yet be ready for prime time. San Diego's Jim O'Neil, a distance runner who has competed in all 22 U.S. and eight world meets for masters, joked about the Mayor's request: "First, everybody from Eugene stood up. Then, everybody who couldn't understand English stood up." Still, nobody could deny the local enthusiasm. "We've never come close to seeing this level of support before," conceded O'Neil. At the opening ceremonies, as waving athletes marched around the track to continuous applause, tears filled many eyes. It was a stunning acclamation to the vigor of a group of track and field warriors who refuse to age.

When in 1986, Eugene bid to be first U.S. city to hold the biennial world track and field meet for masters, organizers Tom Jordan and Barbara Kousky pegged their approach on Eugene's reputation as "track capital of the U.S." They got the meet, and three years of organizational headaches, but in truth, Eugene's reputation lately had begun to tarnish. Formerly training base for many of America's running elite, the logging and college town probably now ranks behind Boulder, Houston and Santa Monica. The once pre-eminent Nike/O.T.C. Marathon no longer serves as "a gathering of eagles." Through a combination of rising ticket prices and ennui, neither the Prefontaine Classic nor Oregon dual meets attract the capacity crowds of old. Resident Joe Henderson explains, "The aging joggers on the sawdust trails don't identify with young racers any more."

The gap between joggers and masters elite seemed easier to bridge. Thus, on a cool Thursday evening in late July, both groups jammed downtown Eugene to either participate in, or spectate at, a 10 Km road race that (following a day of heptathlon and decathlon competition) served to open the meet of masters. Nearly a thousand ran. Alan Roper and Peter Jones, both from Great Britain, broke away from Belgium's Omer Van Noten in the last mile. Roper's winning M40 time: 30:43.40. Bronwen Cardy-Wise of Great Britain, W35, led all women with 34:00.60.

But you had to look deep in the field for some even more remarkable performances. New Zealand's Ron Robertson placed fourth overall with 30:53.80, winning M45. New Zealand's Roger Robinson ran 32:13.90 for a ten-second victory over Ireland's James McNamara, who later would catch him in the track 10,000. Norm Green, a Baptist minister from Wayne, Pennsylvania, won M55 in a world's best 33:09.50, then two days later ran a track world record 33:00.66. Clerics seemed to predominate at that age level. Sister Marion Irvine, W55, rejoiced when she crossed the line in 39:59 on the finish-line clock, later adjusted to a humbler 40:01.10, still a world best. Irvine, a Dominican nun and school principal from Napa, California, eventually earned five individual gold medals, including a cross country race that (in best Oregon fashion) featured a log barrier that almost halted her. "I went over hands and knees to be safe," she said.

Robinson, however, provided the best laugh of the meet at a mid-week clinic. He noted that while most Americans use the term "masters" for athletes over 40, the international expression is "veterans." Robinson once ran a road race in Kansas City. Catching an athlete he suspected of being in his age group, Robinson asked, "Are you a vet?"

"No," came the answer. "I'm an accountant."

Meeting in Eugene, the World Veterans' Athletic Association (W.A.V.A.) rejected a proposal to become masters instead of vets. The international organizing body also delayed a vote to equalize the age at which male and female vets can compete. Originally, women were allowed to start at 35 (as opposed to 40 for men) as a form of encouragement, but with one third of the competitors in

Eugene female, that need seemed past. "The age difference makes it seem we grow older sooner than men, which is not the case," says Joan Ullyot, M.D., W45 cross country bronze medalist from San Francisco.

Women, of course, competed in the 10,000 and marathon at the World Vets well before they could in the Olympics. In Eugene, women vets also competed for the first time in the triple jump, pole vault, hammer throw and 2000 meter steeplechase. Eyeing the future, the International Amateur Athletic Federation (I.A.A.F.) requested a report on how they did. Some day we may see those events in the Olympics, if it seems feasible that young females can do the same as their elders.

From the beginning, W.A.V.A.'s founders sought to avoid the political problems that often beset international athletics. Thus the World Vets opening ceremony features a march behind age-group signs rather than flags. Some competitors compete in national uniforms; most do not. If anybody has tallied medals won, their count has remained, refreshingly, unpublished. No restriction is made on the number that can enter from any one country, and although there are "suggested" standards for each event, anyone wishing entry can ignore them. (Founder Dave Pain, whose sore knees prevent him from running regularly, took more than an hour to finish the 10 Km cross country race and still beat three in his M65 division.) Professional athletes were welcomed from the beginning; so were South Africans (black and white), despite that nation's ban from the Olympic movement. In 1989, athletes from the Soviet Union competed for the first time. Janis Zirnis won the M40 javelin in 71.10 meters (233 feet 3 inches). Taisija Tsentsik, Olympic bronze medalist from 1964, won the W50 high jump, clearing 1.45. "We're just getting started," admitted Vadim Marschev, an M50 sprinter. "We held our first veterans' meet in Moscow three years ago. We had 300 in March at our first indoor championships." Marschev ran sixth in a 200 heat, failing to make the finals. W.A.V.A. president Cesare Beccalli hailed the Soviet presence as signalling "a new era in veterans' activity."

Alas, W.A.V.A. (which functions on a slender $40,000 annual budget) has not entirely succeeded in keeping politicians at bay. When it seemed likely that the I.A.A.F. might establish a rival veterans' organization, W.A.V.A. reluctantly agreed to bar South Africans. Two groups from India appeared in Eugene (one Hindus, the other Sikhs), each claiming pre-eminence. W.A.V.A. asked them to work out their differences through the I.A.A.F.

Vets also have agonized over cheating. Two American athletes–one a hurdler, one a decathlete–were back in competition in Eugene after having served suspensions for falsifying their age. One American athlete had consistently outjumped a European rival for most of the last decade, their performances declining equally with age. Suddenly, the European improved, winning in Eugene. The American wonders whether his rival is training harder, or possibly using steroids. "The problem is real," concedes Sheahen, who serves as W.A.V.A. treasurer, "but testing athletes in so many age categories would prove enormously expensive."

Cost of the 1989 World Vets meet was $900,000, half coming from entry fees. After San Diego lost the bid to Eugene, David Pain headed a fund drive that raised $75,000 in donations from American competitors. The rest of the money came from sponsors, including Weyerhaeuser, Nike, United Airlines and Hewlett-Packard. Nobody showed any interest in televising the World Vets, even for free.

If anyone made money, it might have been a promoter from the Far East. Fifty-nine athletes from an Asian country entered The Athletics Congress Masters Championships in San Diego that served as a prelude to the World Vets. Surprisingly, most were female, and none showed. Later, rumors circulated that someone had been selling entries into the masters meets for $100 as a ploy to avoid visa restrictions. The U.S. Embassy, however, refused to issue visas.

Most competitors, however, arrived with proper documents and loftier goals, even if their goal was only sightseeing. In San Diego, New Zealand's Derek Turnbull, M60, won the 5000 in the morning, spent four hours with his wife at Sea World, then returned late afternoon to set a world 1500 record, 4:29.11.

Turnbull, a sheep rancher who claims to train only twice weekly and gather strength shoving ewes around, bettered that mark winning the 1500 in Eugene (4:28.66) and also claimed gold medals in the 800 and marathon as well as the three 10 Km races: road, track and cross country. His total was six. Nevertheless, competition has improved so significantly in the older divisions that even Turnbull got shoved around in the 5000, going out too hard in the first mile, then crumbling to the relentless pursuit of Italy's Cesare Bini. Roger Robinson found the race both memorable and amusing: "The Italians in the stands were screaming, *E' morto! E' morto!* 'He's dying! He's dying!' Bini kicked and won the race. Derek was trying so hard, he spat out his false teeth, turned around, picked them up, and still got second."

Another multiple gold medalist from Down Under, Australian John Gilmour, M70, also suffered a rare defeat. After winning a morning 5000, Gilmour allowed Daniel Bulkley of Phoenix, Oregon to establish a long lead in the 800 finals that evening. On the final stretch, Bulkley began to buckle, Gilmour bearing down. But as Gilmour surged past to claim what seemed an inevitable victory, Bulkley recovered and nipped Gilmour at the line.

Many well-known American masters remained home, apparently preferring road race cash to medals around the neck, but the World Vets was not without celebrities. Kenya's Kip Keino, 1968 Olympic champion at 1500 meters, steeplechase winner in 1972, carried the torch at the opening ceremonies, but failed to make the finals of the M45 1500 meters. Four-time Olympic champion Al Oerter won the lightened M50 discus in 62.74 meters (about 200 feet). Eddie Hart, best remembered for missing his 100 heat at the 1972 Olympics, showed up on time to win that M40 event (10.87) plus the 200. Larry Walker, bronze medalist in the 50 Km Walk at the same Games, won the M45 20 Km Walk. Bob Richards, two-time Olympic pole vault champion, dropped out of the decathlon injured after four events, then got second in the M60 pole vault. A spectator approached Richards: "You were my boyhood hero. I used to collect Wheaties cereal boxes."

"How old are you?" asked Richards.

"Forty-five."

"I knew it. No one any younger remembers me."

Few who attended Saturday's climactic day of individual track competition would forget the M40 finals at 400 meters with James King of San Diego chasing Stan Whitley of Alta Loma, California through two turns, finally passing on the last straightaway. King ran 48.44 to Whitley's 48.87. Nor would they forget the 1500 races, 17 in all, women followed by men, age followed by relative youth, with barely time for spectators to catch their breaths, or Al Sheahen to finish introductions, between end of one and start of next.

Among the most stirring 1500s was W55, featuring Sister Marion Irvine, wearing a white singlet and shorts best described as properly papal purple. With loping stride and forward lean, Irvine trailed at the half, ten meters down, fifth, seemingly out of contention. But one lap to go, she moved into second, caught Canada's Jean Horne on the final turn, and powered past, raising her arms in victory five meters from the line in a pose reminiscent of Carl Lewis.

By the time of the last and fastest 1500 meters, it was 8:50 P.M., the sun set, the night darkening. Hayward Field is lit only by scattered spotlights, offering a checkerboard of illumination around the track. The dozen M40 finalists preparing to start on the back straightaway–perhaps the greatest field of masters milers assembled anywhere–were indistinguishable, a final gathering of greyhounds.

But few mistook the athlete who seemed to burst from the pack, breaking contact in the first 200 meters. Announcer Sheahen identified him as, "...the great Wilson Waigwa!" Again the staccato applause: Clap! Clap! Clap! Clap! Clap! Four hundred and fifty finals, 2000 medals awarded, and the appetite of Eugene's track fans was not yet whetted.

Waigwa reached 400 in 61.4, then picked up the pace to an 800 in 2:00.50, coincidentally only a tenth of a second slower than Alan Bradford had won the M50 800. Sheahen didn't need to mention it. The thought was in everyone's mind, even though the distance was metric: four-minute mile pace. *Clap! Clap! Clap! Clap! Clap!*

On the back straightaway, Waigwa seemed but a dancing silhouette 20 meters ahead of his nearest rival, Larry Almberg of Ellensburg, Washington. Almberg had a best mile of 4:13, achieved his freshman year at Washington State University. After 21 years away from track miles, he had made his switch back from road racing only two months earlier. But all eyes were on Waigwa, the rabbit on a rail ahead of the greyhounds. Waigwa slowed to 3:03.21 at 1200, but the crowd rumbled to its feet. CLAP! CLAP! CLAP! CLAP! CLAP!

Oh, it was marvelous. Their applause lit the night. And then it was done: a world record 3:49.47. (Almberg claimed an American mark with 3:53.18.) The spectators sighed contentedly and headed for their cars. The athletes lingered on the infield, as though unwilling to abandon their arena to younger and faster, though no less abler, heroes.

There would be a marathon Sunday, and relays, and more marching with music, and speeches, and tears, but despite what everyone conceded was the best-ever World Vets–"Tens," bubbled racewalker John Kelly, "nothing but tens"–thoughts already had begun to turn to Turku, Finland, site of past world records by John Landy in the mile, Emil Zatopek at 10,000, Ron Clarke at 10,000, birthplace of *Paavo Nurmi!* And two years hence in 1991, home, deliciously, of the next World Veterans' Games.

It was enough to make a vet want to live forever.

Appendix: SOURCE LIST FOR MASTERS RUNNERS

Where do you get information on training and racing? The keys to the door of masters track and field can be found below. Essential to any masters athlete is a subscription to *National Masters News*. Membership in T.A.C. is necessary if you expect to compete. Distance runners certainly should read *Runner's World*; athletes in other events, *Track & Field News* if only to keep up with current methods. Finding a coach is difficult for many athletes out of school, particularly masters. A few do exist. The book you have in your hand is the first comprehensive guide for masters runners. Others certainly will follow. Following are some sources to get you started—and keep you going—in masters track.

BOOKS:

How They Train: Long Distances, by Jack Pfeiffer ($7.95). Also: *How Road Racers Train*, by Greg Brock ($8.95); *Runners & Other Dreamers*, by John L. Parker, Jr. ($9.95); and other books on distance running sold by Parker out his back door. Clearwinds Publishing, P.O. Box 13618, Tallahassee, FL 32317; (800) 548-2388.

Masters Age Records. Men's and women's world and U.S. age bests for all track and field events, age 35 and up; racewalking events, 40 and up. Compiled by Peter Mundle, W.A.V.A. and T.A.C. Masters Track & Field Records Chairman. $4.00 plus postage from: National Masters News Order Dept., P.O. Box 2372, Van Nuys, CA 91404. Also: *Masters Track & Field Rankings* ($5.00); *Masters Age-Graded Tables* ($5.95); *Masters 5-Year Age-Group Records* ($1.50); *Competition Rules for Athletics* ($9.95) and other publications.

Masters Running. Bill Rodgers and Priscilla Welch offer advice on what the title says with a strong assist from *Runner's World* columnist Joe Henderson. To be published Fall 1990 by Rodale Press, 33 East Minor Street, Emmaus, PA 18098.

Nancy Clark's Sport Nutrition Guidebook. Subtitled: Eating to Fuel Your Active Lifestyle. Not specifically aimed at masters athletes, but Clark, author of *The Athlete's Kitchen*, offers sound eating advice. ($12.95) Human Kinetics Publishers, Inc., Box 5076, Champaign, IL 61825-5076; (800) 747-4457; (800) 334-3665 (Illinois).

CAMPS:

Florida Runners Camp, 1447 Peachtree Street, N.E., Suite 804, Atlanta, GA 30309; (404) 875-6987. Roy Benson, director. This distance running camp's name is "Florida," but it's held in Brevard, North Carolina with a director who lives in Georgia. Benson began the camp in 1973 while track coach at the University of Florida and simply has retained its familiar name. Three weeks in July ($395 a week), the first specifically geared to "Adults & Triathletes."

Green Mountain Running Camp, 2434 Hawthorne Drive, Yorktown Heights, NY 10598; (914) 962-5238. John Holland, director, along with Benson (above). Lyndon State College in Lyndonville, Vermont in August.

Maine Running Camp, P.O. Box 571, Alfred, ME 04002; (207) 324-0421 (evenings). Andy Palmer organizes this camp for distance runners out of Bar Harbor, Maine.

Mammoth Athletics Camp, Inc., 7411 Earldom, Playa del Ray, CA 90239; (213) 281-1993. John Cosgrove. Plans undetermined as of publication date.

Jeff Galloway's Running Vacations,, P.O. Box 76843, Atlanta, GA 30358; (404) 875-4268. Jeff Galloway, author and member of the 1972 Olympic team, hosts adult distance runners at camps in Atlanta (during Peachtree Road Race), Lake Tahoe, North Carolina and Switzerland. Also running tours to the Bahamas, Florida, etc.

American Racewalk Camp. (See: Organizations.)

COACHES:

Roy Benson, 1447 Peachtree Street, N.E., Suite 804, Atlanta, GA 30309; (404) 875-6987. Former track coach, University of Florida, and director, Atlanta Track Club. Works with runners, middle distance to the marathon, for $60 an hour. Initial visit in Atlanta, or he'll fly to your home, with follow-up by mail and phone.

Ken Martin (APEX Health & Fitness), 106 Candelario, Santa Fe, NM 87501; (505) 988-3122; FAX: 505/982-2599. America's fastest marathoner in 1989 with 2:09:38 at New York; twice winner at Pittsburgh. Coaches by FAX: $45 monthly for workouts sent biweekly. (You tell Ken what you ran the last two weeks, he tells what to run the next two.)

Laszlo Tabori, 10837 Franklin Avenue, Culver City, CA 90230; (213) 837-4794; 478-1057. Member of the 1956 Hungarian Olympic team (4th, 1500 meters); protege of Mihaly Igloi. Coaches Los Angeles Valley College and also the San Fernando Valley Track Club, including masters runners.

Al Lawrence (Endurance Fitness Consultants), 2102 Shiveley Circle, Houston, TX 77032; (713) 590-3515. Bronze medalist at 10,000 meters in the 1956 Olympics. Most of his clients are 40-plus distance runners, although handles a few younger sprinters. Coaches at a local track in Houston, although by correspondence with a few clients.

John Smith, 5146 Ona Crest Drive, Los Angeles, CA 90043; (213) 447-0156. Former world-class 400 meter runner. Assistant coach at U.C.L.A. Also works with runners out of college, including masters.

Mike Barnow, P.O. Box 56, Irvington, NY 10533 (914) 591-5270. Coaches Pace University, but his main love is the Westchester Track Club, open as well as masters. Runners 40 and up, mostly local, but a few by phone and mail as far away as California.

EQUIPMENT:
Eastbay Running Store, Inc., 427 Third Street, Wausau, WI 54401; (800) 826-2205. Running shoes and apparel.

Elite Sales Inc., Box 345, Accord, MA 02018; (617) 749-4389; (800) 433-0324. Primarily a supplier of weight training equipment for Power and Olympic lifters, but Elite also offers shoes for events such as the steeplechase, high jump and javelin, not always available at your local sporting goods store.

M-F Athletic Company, P.O. Box 8090, Cranston, RI 02920-0188; (800) 556-7464. Poles, javelins, hammers, shots, etc. Want a pole vault pit for your back yard? M-F will sell you one for $3795.

Stackhouse Athletic Equipment, Inc., P.O Box 12276, Salem, OR 97309; (503) 363-1840. The official supplier of track and field gear for the 1989 World Vets, Stackhouse carries a complete line of weight implements for masters athletes.

MAGAZINES:
National Masters News, P.O. Box 2372, Van Nuys, CA 91404; (818) 785-1895. Al Sheahen, Editor and Publisher. The official world and U.S. publication for masters track & field, long distance running and racewalking. One year, $22.00. Tabloid newspaper format. Full and gritty coverage of track and field events and road races for athletes over 40. Calendar, results, lists, lively opinions both in columns and in letters to the editor. Masters track might still survive in the U.S. without *NMN*, but it would be less lively.

Runner's World, 33 East Minor Street, Emmaus, PA 18098; (215) 967-5171. Amby Burfoot, Executive Editor. One year, $24. Slick magazine coverage of the sport of jogging, running and racing. Mostly distance oriented, but some track and field. Articles on diet and training often are read by athletes in other sports looking for performance tips. Limited calendar and results. Equipment reviews, latest fashions, pasta recipes, you name it. Technical Editor Mike Tymn writes a column on masters running that appears three times yearly; Senior Writer Hal Higdon often writes on masters topics. *RW* is aware of its aging audience and slants at least some of its coverage to the over-40 crowd.

Running Times, 9171 Wilshire Blvd., Suite 300, Beverly Hills, CA 90210; (213) 858-7100. Ed Ayres, editor and publisher. One year, $19.95. Road racing only. Calendar and results on several hundred races monthly. Not as polished as its big-bucks rival *Runner's World*, but if you want to know who placed first in your age group in races 1,000 miles away, you can't survive without this publication. Annual ranking of age-groupers.

Track & Field News, 2570 El Camino Real, Suite 606, Mountain View, CA 94040; (415) 948-8188. Bert Nelson, Editor. One year, $27.50. "The Bible Of The Sport Since 1948." Only token road coverage and don't expect anything about masters except those few still able to compete with open athletes, but otherwise covers track like a blanket. Sponsors spectator tours to the Olympic Games and other world events. You need a magnifying glass to read lists and results, but *T&F News* offers an important source for literature on technique, particularly for athletes in events ignored by the distance-oriented press.

Veteran Athletics, 67 Goswell Road, London EC1, England. The newspaper for Britain's vets at $20 a year, $30 by air.

ORGANIZATIONS:

American Racewalk Association, P.O. Box 18323, Boulder, CO 80308-8323; (303) 447-0156. Viisha Sedlak, president. An educational organization for anyone who uses the racewalk technique for fitness or competition. Membership of $25 a year includes quarterly newsletter. Sponsors training camps, within and without the U.S.

The Athletics Congress, 200 S. Capitol Avenue, Suite 140, Indianapolis, IN 46625; (317) 261-0500. The National Governing Body for track and field within the United States. Affiliated with the International Amateur Athletic Federation. Masters chairpersons: Track & Field: Barbara Kousky, 5319 Donald Street, Eugene, OR 97405. Long Distance Running: Charles Des Jardins, 5428 Southport Lane, Fairfax, VA 22032. Race Walking: Bev LaVeck, 6633 N.E. Windemere, Seattle, WA 98115. Usually known as T.A.C., or TAC, pronounced "tack," this organization sponsors national championships, including indoors and outdoors for masters. Athletes competing in any TAC event (or in many major road races) need membership in their local association (cost varies). Addresses available from national headquarters.

Road Runners Club of America, 629 S. Washington Street, Alexandria, VA 22314; (703) 836-0558. Executive director: Henley Gibble. The R.R.C.A.'s 456 clubs with 150,000 members organize most of the road races in the U.S. and exert an important, if mostly benevolent, influence on the sport of distance running. Members receive quarterly publication, "Footnotes." Affiliated with T.A.C. Looking for a club in your area? Contact R.R.C.A.

TACSTATS, 7745 S.W. 138th Terrace, Miami, FL 33158; (305) 253-8448. Basil and Linda Honikman serve as the official number-crunchers (i.e., record-keepers) for long distance running within the U.S., publishing *TACTimes*, six times a year (free to athletes and officials). They also offer annual rankings and records for races 5 Km and up ($35 a set, $5 per distance). Also: *Long Distance Running News*, which offers information on T.A.C. programs, people and championships.

U.S.R.A. Masters Circuit, 400 N. New York Avenue, Suite 102, Winter Park, FL 32789; (407) 647-2918. Director: Dean Reinke. Organizes a series of road races offering prize money and focused on masters competition. Also publishes an annual, *Masters Running*.

U.S. National Senior Olympics, 14323 S. Outer Forty Road, Chesterfield, MO 63017; (314) 878-4900. B. L. Bearman, executive director. Sponsors a biennial national competition (same year as World Vets, below) for athletes over 55 in multiple sports including most track and field events. Competitors must qualify via state or regional meets.

World Association of Veteran Athletes. The organization that supervises masters track and field and road racing at the international level. Affiliated with the I.A.A.F. Organizer of the biennial Worlds Veterans' Championships, held in odd-numbered years. President: Cesare Beccalli, Via Martinetti 7, 20147 Milan, Italy; Executive Vice President: Bob Fine, 4223 Palm Forest Drive, Delray Beach, FL 33445; North American Delegate: David Pain, 5643 Campanile Way, San Diego, CA 92115. More managerial than informational; the best source for news on W.A.V.A. events is *National Masters News* (See: Magazines.)

SUPPLEMENTS:

Sleaze, Shortcut Products, Inc., P.O. Box 69, Purgatory, CA 91404; (800) USE-DRUG. President: Herman Teuffel. A natural anabolic product guaranteed to increase energy and performance. Undetectable by present drug tests. Double money-back offer for men whose testacles atrophy or women who grow hair on their chests. Month's supply of 60 pills, or one baseball-sized tablet for those with strong constitutions, $789.95. Also publishes: *How to Cheat in Road Races*.

TECHNIQUE:

Mac Wilkins Productions, P.O. Box 28836, San Jose, CA 95159; (408) 358-2669. Video teaching tapes featuring: Mac Wilkins (discus), Yuriy Syedikh (hammer), Tom Petranoff (javelin), Al Feurbach (shot), Willie Banks (triple jump), priced between $49.50 and $68.00 plus shipping. *Videosports Productions*, P.O. Box 1735, Boulder, CO 80306. Video by masters coach Scott Sanders: "Mastering The Sprints."

Track Management Systems, Inc., 129 Wheeler Avenue, Los Gatos, CA 95032; (800) 553-2188. The "Challenge Form" series of instructional videos for track and field: sprints, distance, race walking, hurdles, triple and long jump, high jump, pole vault, discus, shot, javelin and hammer at $49.95 plus shipping.

TOURS:

Marathon Tours, 108 Main Street, Boston, MA 02129; (617) 242-7845. Thom Gilligan organizes tours to a dozen races, mostly marathons, including Bermuda, London, Stockholm and Athens. Also triathlon and ski trips.

Roadrunner Tours, 2815 Lake Shore Drive, Michigan City, IN 46360. Hal Higdon leads tours to Honolulu, Bermuda and other events (including World Vets) when the spirit moves him.

Sportstravel International, P.O. Box 7823, San Diego, CA 92107; (619) 225-9555. Helen Pain has been organizing tours to masters events since 1972. S.T.I. will attend the 1990 North American Regional Championships in Port of Spain, Trinidad and the 1991 World Vets in Turku, Finland.

Turku '91, Box 10825, Eugene, OR 97440. Tom Jordan and Barbara Kousky, directors of the 1989 World Vets, plan to lead a tour to the 1991 event.

ACKNOWLEDGMENTS

You would not now have this book in hand were it not for the support and encouragement of Al Sheahen, publisher and editor of *National Masters News*. But the book's genesis actually precedes the telephone conversation mentioned in Al's introduction.

Originally, I had been approached by a New York agent interested in having me write a book for a major publisher. The publisher thought that those individuals who had made Jim Fixx's "The Complete Book of Running" a best-seller a dozen years ago might now be in the market for a book aimed at runners over 40.

Maybe so, but it soon became apparent that the book planned by the publisher was not the book I wanted to write. Although the publisher offered a reasonable advance, I eventually declined. The project passed to another writer.

It was soon afterwards that Al and I had our conversation. Al had some previous experience in publishing books privately, including one on economics as well as various record books of interest to masters runners. I sent Al a copy of the outline originally written for the major publisher. Al liked my approach, so we agreed to publish the book together. Although our original intent was to have the book ready for sale at the 1989 World Veterans' Championships, both the writing and publishing tasks proved more formidable than expected. The result is both a better book and one in which I draw upon the experience of Eugene.

This is not the first time I have written for masters runners. My previous "Fitness After Forty' was addressed to them among a broader audience. I also have written about "masters" and the subjects of aging, health and fitness for many national magazines. In preparing this book, I have drawn upon research and writings previously published in magazines that include *The Walking Magazine, Bicycle Guide* and *Physician's Sportslife*.

But I'd like to specifically acknowledge the help of editors at three publications. First is *Runner's World*, whose Executive Editor Amby Burfoot has been both a friend and confidant. I value my connection as Senior Writer for that publication and the opportunity Amby and publisher George Hirsch offer me each month to talk to 445,000 readers and runners.

Thanks also to Bard Lindeman, the former editor of *50 Plus* (renamed *New Choices* after being acquired by *Reader's Digest*). I served Bard as a Contributing Editor, working closely with him and Executive Editor John Tarkov. Among our most worthy projects was producing *50 Plus's* annual All-American team.

I also served as a Contributing Editor for *American Health*, whose Executive Editor Paul Perry served as mentor both for me and for my second son David, who worked at the magazine between stints at *The Runner* and *Tennis*, where he is currently Senior Editor. Dave understands editing better than his father, so he provided important editorial suggestions, reading the manuscript several times during the writing process.

With the book in print, I plan to call on my daughter, Laura Sandall, whose skills at public relations will be helpful in bringing the book to the attention of the public. If we sell enough copies, I'll then turn to my son Kevin and his wife Camille, both certified public accountants. They do my taxes. Obviously, I can't thank them without also thanking my wife Rose, who patiently accompanies me to many masters track meets and road races. She is looking forward to Turku in 1991.

Thanks also to Judy Roseman of Secretary Plus® in Lincolnshire, Illinois. Judy does the secretarial work for the Chicago chapter of the American Society of Journalists and Authors, of which I am president, and I was able to convince Al to let her do the typesetting for this book. It was a wise decision, since she didn't complain once when we kept changing type styles and page numbers.

Les Kidd of Dayton, Ohio designed the cover and, inadvertently, supplied the final name for "The Masters Running Guide." I first spotted Les's work when he won the contest to redesign the logo for the Road Runners Club of America and asked him to design t-shirts for the cross country team I coach in Michigan City. Les did such a good job, I next hired him to design our book cover. Originally I had titled my work in progress "The Master Book." The book was even identified by that title in some preliminary ads. Al wasn't fond of that title and preferred the logical "Masters Running"–except the publisher mentioned earlier chose that as the title for its book. Al and I finally agreed on "Masters Running Guide," except when Les executed his sample sketches, he somehow converted the book to "The Masters Running Guide." It looked good, so Les's title stands.

Photographer Vic Sailer of Rockville Center, New York provided the picture of me finishing at the ICI/USA TAC National Masters Grand Championships in Naples, Florida for the back cover. Printing of the book was done by McNaughton & Gunn in Ann Arbor, Michigan under the supervision of Nancy Compton.

Hal Higdon
Michigan City, Indiana

ABOUT THE AUTHOR

Hal Higdon quit his job as a magazine editor in 1959 and has worked full-time as a freelance writer ever since, selling articles to magazines as diverse as *National Geographic* and *50 Plus*. He serves as Senior Writer for *Runner's World*. He's written two dozen books, including "The Horse That Played Center Field," made into an animated film by ABC-TV. In 1986, he was one of 40 finalists in NASA's Journalist-in-Space program, discontinued after the Challenger explosion.

He began running in 1947 when he went out for his high school track team. Between 1952 and 1968, he participated in six Olympic Trials. He was the first American finisher in the 1964 Boston Marathon, placing fifth. When he won the 10,000 meter race at the A.A.U. masters meet in San Diego a few days after turning 40, he became the first runner to win national titles at the junior, open and masters level.

He set world records in the 3000 meter steeplechase twice (M40, M45) and also won that event twice at the World Vets (1975, 1977). He won the M45 marathon title in 1981. He once held the American open record for the One Hour Run and has set dozens of American age-group records, including one for the 30 Km (M40) broken only recently after 16 years in the books.

Hal Higdon lives in Michigan City, Indiana with his wife Rose. They have three children. Kevin, chief financial officer for Hyde Park Hospital in Chicago, qualified for the 1984 Olympic marathon trials. David, co-captain of the Kalamazoo College tennis team, is Senior Editor for *Tennis*. Laura Sandall is public relations manager for Marshall Field's, the Chicago department store.